Education Policy, Space and the City

Routledge Research in Education

For a full list of titles in this series please visit www.routledge.com

Education Policy, Space and the City

Markets and the (In)visibility of Race

Kalervo N. Gulson

Routledge
Taylor & Francis Group
New York   London

First published 2011
by Routledge
270 Madison Avenue, New York, NY 10016

Simultaneously published in the UK
by Routledge
2 Park Square, Milton Park, Abingdon, Oxon OX14 4RN

Routledge is an imprint of the Taylor & Francis Group, an informa business

Typeset in Sabon by IBT Global.
Printed and bound in the United States of America on acid-free paper by IBT Global.

Library of Congress Cataloging-in-Publication Data

Gulson, Kalervo N.
Education policy, space, and the city : markets and the (in)visibility of race / by
   Kalervo N. Gulson.
      p. cm. — (Routledge research in education ; 47)
   Includes bibliographical references and index.
   1. Education, Urban—Government policy—Case studies.   2. Race discrimination—
Case studies.   3. City children—Education—Government policy—Case studies.
4. Urban geology—Government policy—Case studies.   I. Title.
   LC5115.G85 2011
   370.9173'2—dc22
   2010018829

ISBN13: 978-0-415-99556-6 (hbk)
ISBN13: 978-0-203-83967-6 (ebk)

For Kim, Finn, and Kobi

Contents

Figures and Tables

FIGURES

TABLES

Foreword

In the 1980s and into the 1990s, critical social theory rediscovered the study of space. The turn to spatial theory marked the re-appreciation of Lefebvre's (1991) Marxist-inspired work in *The Production of Space* on one side, and Foucault's (1980, 1986) discourse-based theory of space on the other. Key texts, like Mike Davis' (1998) *City of Quartz*, Soja's (1989) *Postmodern Geographies* and later (1996) *Thirdspace*, and Harvey's (1989) *The Condition of Postmodernity*, ushered an intellectual era understood within a theory of space and 'in the space of theory' (Sparke 2005). In other words, as Kalervo Gulson makes clear in this book, it is impossible to understand education outside of a theoretical and spatial orientation. As Althusser (1976) has argued, theory is about marking a new 'position' whereby a different epistemology is produced and a new way of looking at society becomes possible. For Althusser, this was Marx's great achievement insofar as he was able to institute what Althusser's former teacher, Gaston Bachelard, calls an 'epistemological break'. Schools and the organization of cities like London, Vancouver, and Sydney are co-constitutive of one another. School reform is at once city reform because it supplies the future workers that maintain the city, and events like urban revival depend very much on schools in order to disseminate information and garner broad support (Henig et al. 2001). In education, several key essays took up the constitutive power of space (Allen 1999, Gruenewald 2003, Haymes 1995). In particular, both Haymes and Allen's spatial theories of identity were pathbreaking precursors for what would later become a race theory of space and spatial theory of race. With Lipsitz (2007), Gulson argues that a thorough race theory must deal with both the discursive and material marking of space and a spatial theory is at best incomplete without accounting for race. The analysis comes to fruition when Gulson elevates the race and space nexus to its theoretical conclusion, a phenomenon that has received increased attention since post-Katrina in New Orleans (see Buras 2010, Leonardo 2010). So intimate are space and race that they warrant fusion in a single word: *spacerace*.

Race and the city have been concerns of urban sociologists for some time now. In the US, Massey and Denton (1993) have called the spatial concentration of one racial group in 'ghettoized' conditions as 'American Apartheid'. They operationalize *ghetto* as:

> a set of neighborhoods that are exclusively inhabited by members of one group, within which virtually all members of that group live. By this definition, no ethnic or racial group in the history of the US, except one, has ever experienced ghettoization, even briefly. For urban blacks, the ghetto has been the paradigmatic residential configuration for at least eighty years. (Massey and Denton 1993: 18–19)

Spurred on by American industrialization and Black migration from farms to cities, US Black ghettos are a twentieth century creation. Through zoning, streaming, blockbusting, Housing and Urban Development policies, White flight, and a host of ideological manipulations, Black ghettoization in the US became a science. This particular form of Apartheid gave birth to the schools that Black children in the inner cities now attend, giving rise to what Anyon (1997) calls 'ghetto schooling'.

Massey and Denton acknowledge that other ethnic groups, such as Italians, Poles, and Jews, also experienced ghettoization. However, they add that there are several crucial distinctions from Black experience with segregation. First, unlike Black ghettos, White ethnic enclaves were never as homogeneous, hosting a range of immigrant ethnic groups that shared a contiguous space. White ghettos were never just that. Second, most White ethnics across the US did not live in ghettoized conditions in the same manner as Blacks, the latter mirroring Third World conditions. Finally, ghettos have become an almost permanent feature of Black life, whereas White ghettos were much more fleeting. Even the Black middle class is part of the ghetto. White ethnic ghettos became a holding ground for new immigrants who eventually transitioned out of them into increasingly mixed neighborhoods, but the Black ghetto has become a stubborn presence for Blacks who have been US citizens for many generations. Massey and Denton (1993) have a two-step definition of the ghetto as: 1) embodying racial homogeneity; and, 2) housing most members from a particular race within the larger metropolitan area. Thus, this definition prevents an otherwise ridiculous suggestion that White spaces like Beverly Hills or Bel Air are ghettos because while they may meet the first criterion, it is clear that most Whites in Los Angeles do not live in those zip codes.

In a kind of US 'orientalism' (see Said 1978), social scientists have turned the Black ghetto into a controlled place of knowledge, a disciplined space of existence (Kelley 1998, Leonardo and Hunter 2007). The collective Black urban has become largely defined by the White gaze that consumes it as a sign of both decay and utter fascination.[1] Criminalized, foreignized, and abjectified, these collective Black spaces have become not just permanent features of minority lives but of White minds and fantasies as well. They are sites of scapegoating when times are lean; places of vicarious, often sexualized, transgressions; and internal reminders of White superiority and socio-spatial imagination (Dwyer and Jones III 2000). They are never outside of the concept of the 'city limits' because they prop up the image of desirable zip codes, the city's Other within. They are not orientalized through exclusion but precisely through inclusion and participation in city creation. In other words, they are not left up to chance but part of the architecture of city life. They are not the city gone wrong because they were not meant to be right in the first place. Black spaces are perhaps exactly what they were meant to be: forsaken foils to White spaces. They are controlled places of difference that remind us that White spaces exist because of their complement. You cannot have one without the other.

As Gulson shows, the new spacerace is not a reworking of the more traditional concept of segregation. It does not merely indict cities for creating Black and White spaces (this would have been enough). Even in more or less 'integrated' settings, race is still in play, always a factor in how the space is racially marked and made meaningful. In schools and cities that boast less severe segregation patterns, or lower 'dissimilarity index' to use Massey and Denton's (1993) terminology, we find race to be significant. And with the globalization of race underway, there is hardly any space that remains untouched by the long arm of racialization. That said, nowhere is this process more poignantly on display than in big cities, from New York to New Delhi, where immigration and gentrification, extreme poverty and wealth, and difference and xenophobia exist side-by-side in an undeclared war. City schools bear witness to these modern contradictions as the sidewalks and the hallways become one seamless pathway on which kids trudge daily. In a sense, city creation always contains an educative project and education is bound up with a city's future as families move into cities in search of the three primary securities of jobs, housing, and schooling.

It is impossible to understand the evolution of cities without critical appreciation of the continuing reinvention of race. For example, when US Blacks migrated from southern farms to northern cities, they confirmed the place of city life as part of their hopes for a better life. Instead, they were met with riots, daily psychological assaults, and spatial marginalization. When immigrants of colour flocked into the metropolis, they came in search of jobs and social opportunities. They found more than that; Carlos Bulosan's (1973) tale *America is in the Heart* chronicles the cruelties that workers faced in the fields and factories. Today, families continue to eke out new forms of existence and forge new identities in large cities with a population over 10 million and 'small urbans' of a few hundred thousand people centred on colleges and developing industries. Whether we want to call these spatial conditions modern or postmodern, cosmopolitan or evidence of Wal-Martization, we may inquire into what we have made of the city and what the city has made of us to which we no longer consent. That race has something to do with it is indisputable. Whether it has to continue in its present form is the real question.

Zeus Leonardo
University of California—Berkeley

Acknowledgements

In a higher education environment where, increasingly, all that seems to matter is how many articles an academic has in top-quality, spectacularly well-regarded journals, writing a book seems somewhat of an anachronism. However, I like academic books. I like how they look on the shelf, sitting there just waiting to be (incidentally) picked up. I also like what they offer an author: the opportunity to take intellectual risks, to play with uncertainty and unfinished thoughts, to generate ideas in such a way that where a book finishes is perhaps a long way from where it starts.

That said, this is my first sole authored book, and I have realised writing a book should not be, and in fact cannot really be, an isolated undertaking. It is much more fun, far less nerve racking, and substantially more stimulating, to share the joy, fear and risk of writing with friends, colleagues and challenging interlocutors. And thinking and writing is tiring, so sometimes it is just good to have others around. Thus, I would like to thank the following people for getting me through this process.

Amy Metcalfe read every word of this ever-changing tome. Her intellectual acuity and attention to detail was invaluable. And her unfailing belief that this book would be finished, sometimes flying in the face of all available evidence, counted for more than I can express.

Colin Symes read most of this manuscript in various forms and provided, as always, penetrating feedback. I also much appreciated his generous insights into the often unacknowledged affective dimension of writing a monograph.

My thanks to the following who read different parts of the book: Mark Davidson, who supported my desire to use spatial theory, while keeping me from reinventing the spatial wheel; Eva Bendix Petersen, who, as always, challenged me to be attendant to not only substance but style; Robert Parkes, who co-authored some of the original articles drawn on this book and was generous in both allowing me to use these ideas and encouraging me to take them further; and Jessica Ringrose, for her ideas on imaginaries, and without whom I would have written a different Chapter 5. Thank you also to my friends who proofread: Tom Grant, Jason Metcalfe, and David Yule.

My thanks to Deborah Youdell for her feedback on the ideas in this book and encouragement to complete it so I could stop rambling on about space. Thank you also to David Gillborn, who has helped me to understand what it means to do critical policy work and race, within and outside the academy. He is a model of the contemporary public intellectual.

This book would not be written without my commissioning editor at Routledge, Ben Holtzman. Thank you for your belief in me. My present editor, Max Novick, inherited this book from Ben in October 2009 and contacted me immediately as it appeared to be overdue. He received a prompt email from me, telling him it was going to be late. Max, thank you very much for your patience. Thank you also for your guidance in getting this book to completion.

I have spoken about the themes of this book with colleagues and friends in university departments, at conferences and seminars, and in cafes and pubs. Some of the following people will, of course, not agree with what I have written. However, all of them have been generous in challenging my thinking, and thus in shaping this book. My thanks to: Felicity Armstrong, Stephen Ball, Kristen Buras, Tim Butler, Jo-Anne Dillabough, Aslam Fataar, Luis Armando Gandin, Rob Hattam, David Hursh, Nathanael Lauster, Zeus Leonardo, David Ley, Bob Lingard, Pauline Lipman, George Morgan, Tom Pedroni, Michael Peters, Daryle Rigney, Fazal Rizvi, Kjell Rubenson, Claudia Ruitenberg, David Saltmarsh, Sue Saltmarsh, Chris Taylor, Pat Thomson, Taylor Webb, Handel Wright, and Ee-Seul Yoon.

I would also like to thank my friends and colleagues in the Department of Educational Studies, who for two years have been nodding understandingly, and providing encouragement, when I have talked about this book I am writing, finishing, completing, editing.

And I want to finish by thanking my family, including my parents, Brian and Dianne, and my brother Brendan, for their unwavering support over the years. Unfathomable thanks go to my partner Kim, who has lived with the spectre of this book in our home. Thank you for your love, encouragement, and our life together.

Lastly, our son Finn was six months old when, two years ago, Routledge approved the contract for this book. Our son Kobi was born in September 2009. Both boys have taught me that while writing matters (and must be done differently with young kids), what also matters is getting down on the ground, reading books aloud, playing with trucks and dinosaurs, digging in the dirt, and chewing wooden blocks and dolls.

Kalervo N. Gulson
University of British Columbia, 2010

COPYRIGHT ACKNOWLEDGMENTS

Baillie, P. (2004). 'Rubble from the demolition of a drug house is removed from 'the Block', Redfern, Sydney'. Photograph is reproduced with permission of the photographer and the National Library of Australia.

While the majority of the writing in this book is original, portions of this book, and related ideas, have appeared in different form in the following articles and chapters. Thank you to the editors and publishers for permission to reproduce this work.

Gulson, K. N. (2005). Renovating educational identities: Policy, space and urban renewal. *Journal of Education Policy, 20*(2), 141–158.

———. (2006). A white veneer: Educational policy, space and 'race' in the inner city. *Discourse: Studies in the Cultural Politics of Education, 27*(2): 251–266.

———. (2007a). Mobilizing space discourses: politics and educational policy change. In Gulson, K. N. Gulson & Symes, C. (Eds.), *Spatial theories of education: Policy and geography matters* (pp. 37–56). New York, Routledge.

———. (2007b). 'Neoliberal spatial technologies': On the practices of education policy. *Critical Studies in Education, 48*(2): 179–195.

———. (2007c). Repositioning schooling in inner Sydney: Urban renewal, an education market and the 'absent presence' of the 'middle classes'. *Urban Studies, 44*(7), 1377–1391.

———. (2007d). With permission: Education policy, space and everyday globalisation in London's East End. *Globalisation, Societies and Education, 5*(2): 219–237.

———. (2008). Urban accommodations: Policy, education and a politics of place. *Journal of Education Policy, 23*(2), 153–163.

———. (2009). Wither the neighbourhood? Education policy, neoliberal globalisation and gentrification. In Popkewitz, T. & Rizvi, F. (Eds.). *Globalization and the study of education.* Chicago, National Society for the Study of Education Yearbook, Volume 108, Number 2.

Gulson, K. N. & Parkes, R. J. (2009). In the shadows of the mission: Education policy, urban space and the 'colonial present' in Sydney. *Race, Ethnicity and Education, 12*(3), 267–280.

———. (2010a) Bringing theory to doctoral research. In Thomson, P. & Walker, M. (Eds.) *The Routledge doctoral student's companion: Getting to grips with research in education and the social sciences.* London, Routledge.

———. (2010b) From the barrel of the gun: Policy incursions, land and Aboriginal peoples in Australia. *Environment and Planning A, 42*(2), 300–313.

1   Policy, Space, and Theorising the City

> If you ask the people you meet, 'Where is Penthesilea?' they make a broad gesture which may mean 'Here,' or else 'Farther on,' or 'All around you,' or even 'In the opposite direction.'
>
> 'I mean the city,' you ask, insistently.
>
> 'We come here every morning to work,' someone answers, while others say, 'We come back here at night to sleep.'
>
> 'But the city where people live?' you ask.
>
> 'It must be that way,' they say, and some raise their arms obliquely towards an aggregation of opaque polyhedrons on the horizon, while others indicate, behind you, the spectre of other spires.
>
> 'Then I've gone past it without realising it?'
>
> 'No, try going on straight ahead.' (Calvino 1972: 157)

In this passage from Italo Calvino's *Invisible Cities*, young Marco Polo tells an ageing Kublai Khan of his exchanges with inhabitants of the city of Penthesilea. For me the passage invokes two related issues germane to this book. The first is that understanding education policy in the inner city is similar to the traveller's conundrum in locating 'the city'; that is, the difficulty in identifying the boundaries between different types of politics and policies, the broad gestures of ambiguity arising when educational policy converges with other urban policies. The second issue pertains to providing substance to the category 'city', in order to think about the geographies of education policy.

Working from and with these issues, this book is an exploration of the geographies of education policy in the inner city. My substantive argument is that the processes and practices of neoliberal education policy enable the primacy of the white middle classes, as an assemblage of aspiration and idealisation, in inner city public[1] schooling. Furthermore, I contend neoliberal education policy renders race (in)visible, and as such augurs poorly for the future of inner city areas. Education policy thus contributes to constituting and consolidating a white, middle-class (re)imagining of the inner city (cf. Butler and Robson 2003, Ley 1996).

In this book I proffer a specific way to think about education policy. Often understood as being outside the concerns of the city due to its formulation either at a federal or state/provincial level, education policy could conversely be positioned as part of urban policies and the everyday fabric of cities. However, this book does not provide an overview of, or propose solutions to, the myriad problems and issues faced by inner city public schools (e.g., Pink and Noblit 2007). Rather, this book sketches out, and attempts to destabilise, conceptual and empirical understandings of inner city education policy. I posit that previous policy studies of urban schooling have failed, with notable exceptions, to adequately take stock of the constitutive role of the city in the processes and practices of education policy.

I also assert that the processes and practices of education policy are constitutive of contemporary cities, as a way of exploring how '[t]he city is conceptualised explicitly in social theory, implicitly in social policy and routinely in social practice' (Keith and Cross 1993: 7). I am interested in the complex links between schools and the city, and in the multiple and often contradictory ways in which people make decisions about and participate in schooling, whether they be parents, teachers, policy makers, school administrators, or some other interested party. I am thus intrigued by what is possible and not possible, in and of, within and against, the city.

I ground these points about education policy and the city in three case studies of K–12 education policy relating to education markets and the restructuring of schooling, in inner city areas of London, Sydney, and Vancouver. Each urban area of examination is one within which people and schools are under stress, while the areas are simultaneously being transformed through redevelopment and/or policy interventions. The case studies are a combination of unpublished, and published work, that draw on: one, a 2002 to 2004 study, that looked at the interplay of urban renewal, education policy, and identity in Sydney and London; two, ongoing examinations of race, Aboriginality, whiteness, and the city; and three, a 2008 study on education markets and race in Vancouver. (For methodology associated with these studies, see, Gulson 2005, Gulson 2007, Yoon and Gulson, forthcoming).[2] More than merely summation, this relatively short book is intended to be a companion to my previous publications (see Acknowledgements).

The specifics of cities and education policies are important, I think, to counter totalising accounts, such as those associated with certain invocations of globalisation (Smith 2001). However, I am caught in the paradox of case study research, caught in the tensions between the uniqueness of a case and a desire for generalisation. Nonetheless, to 'live with ambiguity, to challenge certainty, to creatively encounter, is to arrive, eventually at "seeing" anew' (Simons 1996: 238). Therefore, my aim in examining three different education and urban policy regimes in three different cities is to identify ethnographically the ways in which education markets unfold in different inner city areas, while also being concerned with conceptualising policy processes and practices. My approach corresponds with a comparative approach premised on 'academic engagements that may be largely ethnographic in nature and rooted in specific sites, but simultaneously invite comparative analysis' (Keith 2005: 2).

Additionally, I explicitly foreground a spatial approach to educational policy studies. In previous work Colin Symes and I argue that:

examining education policy from a spatial perspective is not about creating 'new' problems as such, but rather it is about providing explanatory frameworks that, perhaps, disrupt understandings in, and posit new possibilities for, 'mainstream' education policy studies. (Gulson and Symes 2007: 2)

This book continues this work,[3] drawing at times on previous spatial explorations, and extending them into new territories. I try to write in the spirit of interdisciplinarity, or more precisely what Lefebvre calls 'transdisciplinarity'. Soja defines this as 'not being the privileged turf of such specialized fields as History, Sociology, and Geography, but spanning all interpretive perspectives' (Soja 1996: 6). To give a sense of this orientation, the rest of this chapter outlines some of the conceptual premises that guide, though do not determine, my analyses.

A NOTE ABOUT THEORY AND EDUCATION POLICY

I am interested in the policy and everyday aspects of the city, and I am fascinated by how 'policy is practiced and contested in local sites' (Ball 1994a: 10). I want to deal with, in some sense, the idea that policy is spatial in form and in consequence. I wish to work from Ball's (2006) two key points concerning 'the insularity and abstractness of much education policy research' (p. 18). Ball's first point maintains policy research should to be relocated outside of national boundaries; this point is part of the early call for globalising educational policy studies. Ball's second point pertains to issues about place and the local, in that much educational policy research treats schools as discrete from their physical and cultural locations. Consequently, this research fails to convey precisely where schooling takes place as well as how and why. For Ball (2006), 'this is not simply a point about empirical description, although more of that would be very welcome, it is also about theorisation' (p. 19). This is a challenge and provocation and, in line with my thinking over the past few years, represents a call to (re)examine educational policy in relation to spatiality. This book is thus concerned with how empirical endeavours are guided by and speak to theory, and I work back and forth between empirical description and theorisations of the spatialities of policy.

I want to draw attention to Flyvberg's (2001, following Foucault 1977) assertion that the social sciences are recursive, with humans as both the objects and subjects of study. In this book, theory, especially social and urban theory, and the overlaps herewith, tends to operate as an interpretive device. Ball articulates this work of theory well when he asks:

what is the point of theory? . . . Theory is a vehicle for 'thinking otherwise'; it is a platform for 'outrageous hypotheses' and for 'unleashing criticism'. Theory is destructive, disruptive and violent. It offers a language for challenge, and modes of thought, other than those articulated for us by dominant others. It provides a language of rigour and irony rather than contingency. The purposes of such theory is to defamiliarise present practices and categories, to make them seem less self-evident and necessary, and to open up spaces for the invention of new forms of experience. (Ball 1995: 266)

There are two points to make here (also made previously in Gulson and Parkes 2010a). The most obvious point is theory operates as tool for defamiliarisation, denaturalisation, disaffection, diffraction, and deconstruction. It becomes a means by which to challenge the present by bringing a fresh perspective to the objects of concern. A second point relates to theory as a platform from which to launch critique. Ball's articulation of the work of theory relies on a critical insight of poststructural discourse theory: *the impossibility of making statements outside of discourse*. In practice this means that it is impossible to take a stance on an issue that does not itself situate the speaker in the ambit of a particular theoretical tradition. Thus, within discursive logic, there can be no statements outside of theory. Or, to place a Foucauldian spin on Derrida's (1976) infamous statement, *il n'y a pas de hors-texte*,[4] there is no 'truth' outside of discourse/text, since it is discourse that provides the truth-value of any claim made.

In this book I am working with theory as situated (Gregory 1994), and am perhaps also looking to generate theory, in a similar way to Armstrong's aim to '"seek theory" through the study and application of particular instances in exploring the processes and relationships involved in policy making and spatiality' (Armstrong 2003: 42). However, doing this engenders implicit and explicit contradictions in the capacity to use various theoretical premises that are generated specifically and yet universally applied. Connell (2007) suggests social theory has been dominated by what she calls metropolitan society, or the metropole, which is primarily European and, to a lesser extent, North American. Social sciences had their ostensive origins in metropolitan society, and as such metropolitan theory carries with it the legitimacy of theory generation and exportation. This resonates with Robinson's (2006) discussion of the separation of South African cities from theorising in urban studies, in which she maintains 'poorer cities and marginal cities have been profoundly excluded from the theoretical imaginary of urban modernity' (p. x). A counter suggestion by Connell is 'southern theory' which redefines the margins, both as a geographical and a-geographical marker. For example, the metropolitan world becomes the minority world, and can then be reconstituted as the margins.

Additionally, Gregory's idea of 'working with' theory is useful in thinking about situated theory. He notes that theory:

does not come ready-made. . . . [I]t provides a series of partial, often problematic and always situated knowledges that require constant reworking as they are made to engage with different positions and places. Conceived thus, social theory, like geography, is a 'traveling discourse', marked by its various origins and moving from one site to another. (Gregory 1994: 12)

This leads to an engagement with what Said (1983) identifies as the problems with 'travelling theory', pertaining to the suspect assumption that ideas travel untrammelled. Contiguous with Connell's point about metropolitan theory, Said notes that '[t]heory has to be grasped in the place and time out of which it emerges' (Said 1983: 241–242). Similarly, the ideas in play in this book such as markets, neoliberalism, and space are always provisional and recursive. While I note commonalities in policy processes and practices across the cities of Sydney, Vancouver, and London, I also want to be attendant to the limits of universality. I wish to be attendant to the limits of ethnographic comparison, and the (im)possibilities of 'multi-sited ethnography' (Hage 2005). I am also inclined to think readers of this book will find what Peters and Kessl (2009) note as 'a latent tension between a humanist Marxism and poststructuralism that . . . seems to reflect a larger set of differences not only within geography but social theory itself' (p. 22). Following Soja (1996: 5), I am choosing to let this tension remain, with ideas at times in contradistinction, at times in jarring embrace, while overall, I hope contributing to a sense of epistemological openness.

PUBLIC POLICY AND CRITICAL POLICY STUDIES

In this book I examine what is termed public policy (Anderson, 1984, Dye 1992, Howlett and Ramesh 1995, Pal 1987, Sharkansky 1970), which 'refers to all areas of government action across the spectrum from economic policy to those policies usually referred to under the rubric of social policy, covering education, health and welfare areas' (Taylor et al. 1997: 22). These are policies made by governments, national or state/provincial, in the case of policy relating to education markets, and by federal, state/provincial, and local or municipal governments as is the case for some urban policies such as housing and public amenity. This is not to position policy as a top-down process, but rather that the education and urban policies identified in this book are given the imprimatur of legislative and municipal governments, and involve political actors and state institutions.

Public policy can be seen as 'normative, expressing both ends and means designed to steer the actions and behaviour of people' (Rizvi and Lingard 2009: 4), and as such involves the authoritative allocation of values (Easton 1953). As Rizvi and Lingard note, it is important to recognise the complexity of the relationship between policy and values. While values can be allocated in multiple ways for varying purposes:

> above all, policies are designed to ensure consistency in the application of authorized norms and values across various groups and communities: they are designed to build consent, and may also have an educative purpose. (Rizvi and Lingard 2009: 8–9)

What also needs to be identified is how these values emerge and come to be mobilised, or allocated, through authority (Bacchi 2000). As such I take the position that policy and politics are intricately connected (Lingard and Ozga 2007). This leads to a concern with how power is understood, for different conceptions of power lead to different notions of policy and, consequently, different approaches to policy analysis. With a focus on power, politics, and policy, the approach taken in this book is located within critical education policy studies (Ozga 2000, Taylor et al. 1997). As I outline in Chapter 2, I am adopting a broad *'critical education policy orientation'* (Simons et al. 2009a: 1, original emphasis), drawing on discursive ideas of power, with my analyses located in the field of governmentality studies.

Education Policy, Markets, and Choice

In this book I examine neoliberal policy, and the marketisation of education, broadly understood as the introduction of competition and market-exchange into public education systems (Marginson 1997a). The public schooling systems of Australia (notably New South Wales), England, and Canada (notably British Columbia), have long had some form of educational market, including access to public and private schooling (e.g., Reid 2005), and various forms of public schools (e.g., grammar schools, selective high schools). What changed in the last decade of the twentieth and the first decade of the twenty-first century was that the policy environment not only permitted but actively encouraged education markets.

As a clarifying note, the educational systems dealt with in this book operate as quasi-markets with varying combinations of state control and market mechanisms (Whitty 1997). In Australia, Canada, and the UK, despite significant differences in how educational provision is both governed and delivered, quasi-markets in education are meant to represent and achieve more efficient, competitive, and thus effective schooling, resulting in higher educational standards (Olssen et al. 2004). These markets engender a focus on the role of the individual as a responsible consumer, the constitution of the 'ideal' educational subject, and the processes and outcomes of choice.

It is an established position that proponents of choice in public schooling valorise the consumer. In a schooling context the consumer primarily means parents and, to a lesser extent, students. These consumers are considered to be more knowledgeable about educational choices than educationalists. Educators have a secondary role in the actual choice of school (Olssen et al. 2004).

Additionally, through parental choice it is presumed the market is more effective than state intervention at both increasing performance and achieving social justice (Ball 2008). I will problematise these assumptions throughout the book. The key policy domain referred to in this book, relating to markets and choice, is what is known as open enrolment, which has been posited as a way of ameliorating limitations to educational opportunities for some families (Taylor 2009a). The general principle of open enrolment in a quasi-market is that parents can select any public school for their child but acceptance is decided by individual schools or government agencies depending on the country or state/province in question. Chapters 4 to 6 closely examine inner city markets but for now I will outline the general aspects pertaining to Sydney, Vancouver, and London.

Market Specifics

In Australia, where K–12 schooling is the domain of the states, school choice was historically used to justify government funding for private schools and also to assert more democratic control of schooling (Marginson 1997a, 1997b). In New South Wales, the 1990 *Education Reform Act* was introduced by the Liberal National conservative government. The Act, which was a key move towards open enrolment (Gamage 1992) included partial de-zoning of government schooling through which school attendance, or catchment, areas were retained and schools have to accept any students residing in these areas. However, other students outside catchment areas can apply to attend, and are required to be enrolled, in a public school of choice if there are places (Vinson 2002).

A similar situation occurs in Canada, where schooling is the remit of the provinces. There is a history of education markets in British Columbia (Barman 1991), and the latest iteration came in 2001 when the current Liberal[5] government made changes to the *School Act*. Previous to 2001 students were required to attend the nearest public school as delineated by catchment areas, and, depending on available places, schools would allow students to attend from outside of the area. Post 2001, public schools must continue to accept those students who reside in the attendance area, while other students outside the catchment can apply to attend the school, and are accepted if there is room.

In the UK the Thatcher Conservative government introduced the *Education Act* (1980) and in *Education Reform Act* (1988) to encourage competition between schools, and allow parents to enrol their children in any public school (Olssen et al. 2004). Choice continued to be a component of education policy throughout the Blair and Brown Labour governments. However, what I am most concerned with in relation to the UK is the interplay of marketisation, educational standards, and aspirations in areas where there is little student mobility. This is in order to look at how 'ideal' educational subjects are encouraged by, and constituted in and through, policy.

EDUCATION POLICY AND SPACE

Education policy can be examined as a displaced phenomenon, in which the simultaneity of universal provision with local facilitation of outcomes makes education policy a significant, yet problematic, part of the urban landscape (Lupton 2009). This is further complicated by the introduction of education markets, where 'the social relations arising from market-based relations are dependent upon who and what is included in the spatial organisation of choice' (Robertson 2009: 12). What I think these two points indicate is the need to be cognisant of issues of space in educational research, especially within policy studies.

Spatial theories, when used in educational studies, have primarily been drawn from sociology and the broad field of human geography. Ellsworth notes:

> [a]s an epistemological turn, the spatial turn constitutes a re-direction of attention and a shift in perception that pivots upon this central realization: space is not a neutral setting within which more properly historical processes of struggle, transformation, and reaction play out. (Ellsworth 2008: n.p.)

This 'spatial turn' in education ranges from discussions of school architecture (e.g., Burke and Grosvenor 2008, Ellsworth 2005, Seaborne 1971), power and classrooms (e.g., McGregor 2004), teacher education, pedagogy, and rural and urban education (e.g., Popkewtiz 1998); literacy (e.g., Leander and Sheehy 2004); globalisation, cyberspace, and education (e.g., Usher 2002); and to my areas of interest around education policy (e.g., Armstrong 2003, Thiem 2007, Thomson 2002).

While spatial theories can bring something new to educational policy studies, this book also alludes to, in a small way, how educational research can inform and speak to spatial theories. This aspect has been addressed in recent work by Chris Taylor (2009b) and Thiem (2008), that outlines two dominant themes in spatial approaches to educational research. As Taylor (following Bradford 1990) notes, these themes can be broadly characterised as seeing education and geography as either the *objects* or *subjects* of study. In relation to the latter, 'other social, economic or political processes help understand education and geography better' (Taylor 2009b: 660). It is this type of approach that Thiem (2008) suggests has dominated much education work. This is an inward-looking approach that brings space to bear on educational analyses, yet:

> by positioning the spaces of education as derivative (as in most geographers' work on distribution), or rehearsing familiar arguments about the 'difference that space makes' (the primary claim advanced by educationalists), they do not convey the full potential of education-geographic

research. . . . Most significantly, they neglect education's constitutive properties—that is, how educational systems, institutions, and practices (and the political struggles that surround them) effect change *beyond* the sector. (Thiem 2008: 4, original emphasis)

Taylor (2009b) suggests when education and/or geography are the *objects* of study, ideas emanating from these disciplines are used to examine and understand other social, economic, and political processes. It is this Thiem (2008) calls 'outward-looking analyses' in which geographies of education are 'explanatory moments in their own right. Most outward-looking geographies explore—in some form—how education "makes space", or otherwise contributes to geographical processes' (p. 4). What will become clearer in the course of this book is that I work across both these aspects. Overall, I move towards what Thiem (2007) calls the development of a 'constructivist spatial imagination' in educational policy analyses, a call that Thiem argues is necessarily 'a methodological intervention: if place and scale are part of political practice, they should become part of the conceptual repertoire used to analyze educational governance and policy development' (p. 32). This book then is a small part of developing a spatial imagination concerning cities and education policy.

EDUCATION POLICY AND CONNECTIONS WITH THE CITY

The title of this book, *Education Policy, Space and the City*, echoes an edited collection by Gerald Grace titled, *Education and the City: Theory, History and Contemporary Practice* (1984a). Grace's collection is an attempt to theorise the relationships between schooling and urban settings, working from the premise that studies of urban education had earlier failed to account for urban theory and the structural continuities of the city. As Raffo and Dyson (2007) note, Grace's overall critique continues to be relevant, as 'many educational studies under-theorise the urban, and neglect the ways in which historic structural and economic changes impact on social group cultures and hence on community orientations and aspirations towards education' (p. 265). I address some of Grace's concerns regarding the need for critical scholarship on urban education policy (Grace 1984c), while also approaching policy analysis and the city in a way that departs from Grace's primarily structural theorising of the city (Grace 1984b). In this book, I aim to demonstrate why education is so pivotal to what has happened, and is happening, to cities in the twentieth and twenty-first centuries.[6]

I posit education policy as crucial to understanding the constitutive power of cities. I am concerned with closely connecting an analysis of education policy to other policy realms (Taylor et al. 1997), that circulate and are enacted in the city, to locate education policy within 'more general projects and ideologies of contemporary social policy' (Ball 2006: 19). Anyon (2005a, 2005b) takes this approach when arguing macroeconomic policies are important to understanding why the social justice potential of education is stymied.

Other educational research examines relationships between education, neighbourhoods and demographics. Levin (2009) notes: 'Just as important, but often given less attention in education policy analyses, are events in the larger community, such as changes in employment patterns, migration, urban housing, and social policies' (p. 183). Though it should be noted, there is a long history of geographically oriented studies of the relationships between schooling, community and neighbourhood (e.g., Waller 1937), with an increasing prevalence of studies in the last ten years or so (e.g., Butler and Robson 2001, Power et al. 2002). This book could conceivably be considered part of this rejuvenation of locality studies in education.

Arum (2000) identifies how after a foray in the 1970s into functionalist approaches that dealt with schools in the abstract, as out of place, there has been a renewed interest in place as part of sociology of education. Schools and the immediate surroundings (populations, built environment, etc.) are deemed to be intimately connected, and examining educational achievement (usually posited as academic, and quantifiable, knowledge), requires an understanding of demographics. This has also been the focus of geographers studying education, with work on neighbourhood characteristics and demographic change connected to educational attainment (e.g., Webber and Butler 2007). Related to these endeavours, Raffo and Dyson (2007) suggest work on inequality, urban settings, and education has been characterised by two seemingly incommensurable positions: one, structural readings of social inequality that argue schools are ordered by the same characteristics as society, and thus reproduce inequality; and, two, the ways in which policy interventions into arenas such as parenting are ostensibly able to mediate inequality. Raffo and Dyson argue, with resonance for the aims of this book, that what is required is a middle ground that denotes the spatial and temporal context. What is required is 'an understanding of the specific social and economic dynamics of urban contexts in order to appreciate more fully the cause and consequences of educational inequality in such contexts' (Raffo and Dyson 2007: 265).

A focus of study that links educational inequality and urban contexts pertains to area-based initiatives, common in the UK. These initiatives are organised around the spatial metaphor of 'joined-up' policy making. They have a number of characteristics including: one, are usually targeted at urban areas considered deprived, according to a variety of indices; and, two, an adherence to partnerships, loosely defined and actualised, across agencies, community groups, and the private sector. Education, and particularly elementary and secondary schooling, has been included in area-based initiatives, or education policy has framed area-based initiatives such as *Excellence in Cities* (see Chapter 4).

Area-based initiatives have two key premises. The first is that devolving cooperation to the areas in which services are delivered, and encouraging this cooperation, will address the problems of coordinating multiple government departments and agencies working on the same set of social problems (Cochrane 2007, Power et al. 2005). The second premise is that technical criteria can identify deprivation. Poverty can thus be identified in one place, along with the identification of a 'deprived person' who is also assumed to suffer 'multiple deprivations' (Cochrane 2007).

I should note that the emphasis in this book is not on denoting and/or evaluating educational achievement in area-based initiatives or inner city schools. Rather I am intrigued by the ways education might play an important co-constitutive role with the city (see also Lipman 2007). I see part of this work related to theorising the city, and attempting to think about the city as more than an empty abstract notion to be filled by actors and objects. This is to engage with the material and discursive power of the city in shaping economic, cultural, political, and social relations (see Hubbard 2006).

THEORISING THE CITY

> [T]he city is many things: a spatial location, a political entity, an administrative unit, a place of work and play, a collection of dreams and nightmares, a mesh of social relations, an agglomeration of economic activity, and so forth. (Hubbard 2006: 1)

The ontological status of the city has been extensively examined. One body of inquiry includes what Richard Smith (2007) calls extrinsic approaches, that 'seek to explain the city from without as formed and shaped by exterior forces such as general socio-economic laws (e.g. the forces of capitalism, patriarchy or globalisation)' (p. 260). The introduction of these approaches, such as Castells (1977) *The Urban Question: A Marxist Approach*, was a counter to studies of the urban that gave primacy to the unfettered constitutive power of city inhabitants (see Hubbard 2006 for overview). Conceptual coherence characterise early extrinsic approaches, and others that followed, such as global cities (Sassen 1991) and world cities (Knox 1995). Michael Smith (2001) notes these tend to be neo-Marxist approaches that posit capital and class as the determinants of urban form. This is an approach that underpins, or provides the departure point for, work on gentrification as urban transformation.

Gentrification can be broadly defined as 'the transformation of a working-class or vacant area into middle-class residential and/or commercial use' (Lees et al. 2008: xv). Within the gentrification literature there is a wide range of perspectives from structural theories to theories of consumption, with many debates about the issue of the displacement of the working class from the inner city (Lees et al. 2008). I am interested in two interrelated ideas. The first is the role of policy in encouraging (or discouraging) gentrification, pertaining to what is termed neoliberal urbanism, or 'third wave gentrification'. This involves a 'new amalgam of corporate and state powers and practices' (N. Smith 2002: 443), that spans across planning and social policy realms and is seen to underpin large scale urban development. The second idea relates to the city always in the process of being made, and as such, an approach to gentrification that recognises 'the importance of cultural values and practices as constituents of political and economic life' (Hubbard 2006: 46). This is related to the practices of consumption of those middle classes who choose to live in the inner city, specifically politically progressive individuals and families who refuse the suburban ideal as a model of city life (Ley 1996).

While gentrification is a component of urban change that has some purchase for this book, I do not want to accord it undue conceptual primacy. As a counter-example, all the cities investigated in this book could be considered multicultural cities, with significant histories of immigration. However, I want to remain aware of making arbitrary interventions into complexity. As Keith (2005) notes, in writing about the multicultural city, '[w]e are aware that the very act of description potentially ossifies, and so such a vocabulary needs to be careful about its categoric forms' (p. 11).

Yet the notion of 'the city' is perhaps a necessary heuristic device, and as such I put it forward to provide some indication of the types of readings that underpin this book. As Amin and Thrift note:

> [t]he city has no completeness, no centre, no fixed parts. Instead it is an amalgam of often disjointed processes and social heterogeneity, a place of near and far connections, a concatenation of rhythms; always edging in new directions. This is the aspect of cities that needs to be captured and explained, without a corresponding desire to reduce the varied phenomena to any essence or systemic inquiry. (Amin and Thrift 2002: 8)

I intend to work from and with the sensibility expressed by Thrift and Amin (2002), who further note the 'difference it makes to visualize the city as a process, without the pretence of total sight or generalization' (p. 26). This is also to think about perhaps theory differently, in that the whole of the city's spatiality cannot be captured using one theory or metaphor. This is to proffer what might be called a protean theory of the city.[7] Therefore, in this book I offer relational readings of the city, to examine the interplay of education policy and inner city areas and inhabitants. I do this to explore how schooling forms part of 'a politics of the microspaces of the city' (Amin and Thrift 2002: 158).

UNFINISHED ABUTMENTS

In this book, I am trying to work within and across many areas, sometimes more successfully than others. This is an exploratory as well as explanatory undertaking, and in this task I am encouraged by Foucault who clarifies:

I wouldn't want what I may have said or written to be seen as lay-
ing claims to totality. I don't try to universalize what I say; conversely
what I don't say isn't meant to be thereby disqualified as being of no
importance. My work takes place between unfinished abutments and
anticipatory strings of dots. I like to open up a space of research, try
it out, and then if it doesn't work, try again somewhere else. (Foucault
1994b: 223)

Chapter 2 extends some of the conceptual touchstones noted in Chapter 1,
specifically those dealing with policy and policy analysis. I outline my orientation as a critical policy scholar, linking this to a discussion of Foucault
and policy studies. The latter part of the chapter identifies how governmentality studies provide a related, and productive, way of understanding neoliberal education policy. An important purpose of this chapter is to
demonstrate how policy enables the possible constitution of 'ideal' educational and urban subjectivities in inner city areas.

In Chapter 3 I cover issues of subjectivity, space, and place. I outline
salient understandings of race and class to be applied and rethought
throughout the book. I then move to identify reasons for the 'spatial turn'
in the social sciences, including education. I conclude the chapter by specifying, and illustrating, relational ideas of space and place, premised on
notions of interrelations, multiplicity, and openness, that are then deployed
in Chapters 4 through 6.

Chapter 4 explores the complex connections between Aboriginality,
place, and schooling in Sydney. I examine how education policy positions
gentrification as a positive, yet I note racialised, aspect of urban change.
Gentrification is deemed to import new 'non-Aboriginal' students (the
white middle classes) to the inner city, who will constitute an ostensibly
favourable repositioning of public schooling. I focus on the practices associated with this repositioning, to try to ascertain whether this potentially
reconstitutes Aboriginal students as entrepreneurial subjects.

Chapter 5 connects policy, aspirations, and geographical imaginations
to investigate schooling and place in London. To do this I explore the relationships between two adjacent parts of East London, Canary Wharf (a
financial hub of the city) and Poplar (an area under stress). The chapter
identifies the ways white, middle-class aspirations underscore attempts to
inspire Poplar students to achieve academically. I suggest a form of geographical imagining ties these aspirations to Canary Wharf, and encourages the take-up of desirable neoliberal educational subjectivities

In Chapter 6 I explore the operation of school choice within an inner
city, multicultural neighbourhood in East Vancouver. I identify how the discourses of gentrification, multiculturalism, and the urban edge are drawn
upon by white, middle-class parents to explain residential and schooling
choices. In the latter, race and reputation coalesce to underpin white parents' decisions to send their children to schools other than those they deem
as 'unsafe' or 'unsuitable'. I focus on how school choice inscribes whiteness

in East Vancouver and highlight the problematic nature of discourses of multiculturalism, especially in relation to a white imaginary of the city and the nation.

Chapter 7 concludes the book. In addition to drawing together the empirical chapters with the conceptualisations at play in the book, I suggest neoliberal education policy provides the conditions for increasingly racial-ised inner city areas. Specifically, I draw on the notion of racial neoliberal-ism (Goldberg 2009), and focus on the operation of personal preferences and privatised difference (Brown 2006) to understand the (in)visibility of race in neoliberal education policy. This (in)visibility implicates policy in the constitution and consolidation of neoliberal racisms, through both the (re)inscription of white, middle-class imaginaries, and in the generation of inner cities as discrete, racialised places.

2 Critical Policy Analysis
Governmentality, Rationalities, and Technologies

Critical policy studies have been characterised as a broad 'ensemble of approaches and perspectives' that aim to 'speak truth to power' (Orsini and Smith 2007: 1). This book is a contribution to critical analyses of education policy. It emphasises the interplay of power and politics in the processes and everyday practices associated with education markets in inner city areas. It is also concerned with identifying and conceptualising how education policy connects to urban policy and urban change, including area-based initiatives and gentrification.

In this chapter, I outline my orientation as a critical policy analyst, specifically as a policy theorist. In adopting this approach I accept the act of problematising as a politics, as part of social and policy criticism. I then move to a discussion of Foucault and policy studies, with a focus on critiques of 'micro-political' policy analyses. The latter part of the chapter outlines now governmentality studies complements Foucauldian approaches to understanding policy, which I illustrate through reference to neoliberal educational and urban policy directions. An important purpose of this chapter is to demonstrate how policy enables the possible constitution of 'ideal' educational and urban subjectivities in inner city areas.

CRITICAL POLICY ANALYSIS IN EDUCATION

An important set of critical ideas in education policy studies, arising during the 1980s and 1990s, are those associated with 'policy sociology'. This approach to policy studies adopted theories and methods from sociology and critical social theory (e.g., Ball 1990, Ozga 1987). Part of the development of policy sociology included Bowe, Ball and Gold's (1992) 'continuous policy cycle', or three iterative 'contexts of policy making'. These contexts have some consonance with policy cycle approaches in political science (e.g., Howlett and Ramesh 1995).

Bowe et al.'s (1992) first context is the *context of influence*, in which different groups contest the definition and purposes of education. The second context is *policy text production*, in which texts, including legal texts, policy documents, speeches, and official videos, are read as contested representations of policy. Third is the *context of practice* which denotes the arena where policy issues and solutions are addressed, and where the consequences of policy are experienced. In this arena 'policy is not simply received and implemented . . . rather it is subject to interpretation and then "recreated"' (Bowe et al. 1992: 22). Ball (1994a) added two additional contexts, the *context of outcomes*, which calls for an examination of how policies impact educational and social inequality, and the *context of political strategy*, which identified the need to propose strategies to ameliorate inequalities. These contexts start to call attention to issues of power, contestation and compromise, in relation to education policy. Taken in combination, these five contexts illustrate the dual commitment of critical policy studies in education.

This dual commitment is to understanding policy development in context, and to policy advocacy (Simons et al. 2009a). Advocacy is framed differently from a techno-rational emphasis on improving, evaluating and developing policy, or administration and programmes. Alternatively, critical advocacy is geared towards examining:

> the development of education policy, its content and justifications, the impact of its broader social context and its relation to power and politics in schools. . . . [The] aim is to reveal contradictions, tensions, or general patterns and contingent or structural assemblages. (Simons et al. 2009a: 15)

Like Simons et al. (2009b), I take the position that 'the focus on policy should be regarded as part of the broader interest in power in education and society' (p. 37). Specifically, I understand policy in regard to a broadly poststructural reading of power. Poststructuralism, as a term, has most common use in the North American academy. This term invokes a conceptual and methodological coherence which elides the distinct approaches of theorists such as Derrida, Foucault, and Deleuze (see Peters and Humes 2003). Alternatively, I use the phrase 'discursive readings of power' to delineate the readings most appropriate to my analyses. Specifically, I draw mostly on Foucault's notion of power and discourse which informs a variety of educational policy scholars (e.g., Ball 1994a, Gale 2001, Olssen et al. 2004).

Marxist and liberal policy analysis generally conceive of power as possessed, centralised, and repressive. Conversely, for Foucault, 'power is exercised rather than possessed; . . . power is productive, as well as repressive; and . . . power arises from the bottom up' (Olssen et al. 2004: 24). This alternative conception of power concerns the intersection of power and knowledge, or more accurately power/knowledge. The meanings of and membership within categories of discursive practice will be sites of struggle over power (Clegg 1989). Thus, power constructs 'regimes of truth' (Foucault 1994d). From a discursive position, there:

is a battle 'for truth,' or at least 'around truth'—it being understood
. . . that by truth I do not mean 'the ensemble of rules according to
which the true and the false are separated and specific effects of power
attached to the true,' it being understood also that it's not a matter of a
battle 'on behalf' of the truth, but of a battle about the status of truth
and the economic and political role it plays. (Foucault 1980: 132)

This reading of power informs my orientation as a policy scholar, an orientation distinct from a policy scientist (Ball 1995, Grace 1995, Ozga 2000).
The latter tends to have a techno-rational orientation that includes evaluating existing policies and subsequently developing policy prescriptions.
The former, especially within policy sociology, is more attentive to understanding the contexts of policy development and implementation, while
still plausibly informing policy making (Simons et al. 2009a). My approach
is analogous to that of a *policy theorist* (following Ball 1995). The policy
theorist 'answers to the epistemological challenges of post-structuralism
and the current pluralist social world, and . . . also takes up the difficult
work of intellectually-based social criticism' (Simons et al. 2009a: 27).

However, in the realm of critical policy studies, the policy theorist is
accused of theorising at the expense of action. The commitment to constantly deferred meaning results in charges that policy theorising is sub-
stantively bereft of policy alternatives. As such, this approach is deemed to
have little relevance in the actual field of policy studies. Humes and Bryce
(2003) contend '[i]nevitably, there comes a point of closure and to refuse to
take part in the policy debate is to allow the decisions to be taken by others'
(p. 186). These are pertinent criticisms about the possibilities of the policy
theorist as political agent. Nevertheless, as noted above, the work of the
policy theorist is precisely to destabilise the coherence of decision making
and implementation and to point to the contested, arbitrary, and provisional nature of any policy closure. For me, this undertaking is informed
by Foucault's idea of critique.

> A critique is not a matter of saying that things are not right as they
> are. It is a matter of pointing out on what kinds of assumptions, what
> kinds of familiar, unchallenged, unconsidered modes of thoughts, the
> practices that we accept rest. . . . Criticism is a matter of flushing out
> that thought and trying to change it: to show that things are not as
> self-evident as we believed, to see that what is accepted as self-evident
> will no longer be accepted as such. Practising criticism is a matter of
> making facile gestures difficult. (Foucault 1988: 154, cited in Olssen et
> al. 2004: 40)

To critique as a policy theorist is thus to identify the premises of official
policy discourses and work to actively disrupt the legitimacy apportioned
certain types of knowledge in educational policy change. It is to challenge

assumptions about the logical and coherent processes and practices associated with how policy is framed, how it is made, and how it is taken up. The policy theorist's analytical repertoire can draw on what Bacchi (2000) calls a 'policy-as-discourse' approach. Ball conceives of policy as *text* and policy as *discourse* (Ball 1994a). *Policy as discourse* concerns the production of truth and knowledge; it is 'about what can be said, and thought, but also about who can speak, when, where and with what authority' (Ball 1990: 17–18). This approach is commensurate with theorising in order to defamiliarise, denaturalise, diffract, and deconstruct prevailing regimes of truth in and about education policy, and how practices contingently and provisionally apportion policy legitimacy. To be a policy theorist is, therefore, to take the act of problematising as a politics.

Foucault and 'Micro-political' Policy Studies

Policy analyses in education which draw on Foucault primarily focus on power/knowledge, discourse, and practice. These analyses are often construed as 'micro-political' studies of policy. Notable approaches are policy archaeology (Gale 2001, Scheurich 1994) and policy genealogy (Ball 1994a, Gale 2001), which pay attention to the regimes of legitimacy constituting policy, to contingent power relations, and to inclusions and exclusions (see also Olssen et al. 2004).

However, the very foci of these types of studies are also the locus of criticisms, of which I will touch on three. The first criticism pertains to the relativism ostensibly inherent in any focus on power/knowledge (e.g., Habermas 1987). While not completely rejecting this charge, Olssen et al. (2004) make a distinction between judgemental relativism and epistemic relativism. In relation to the former, judgmental relativism, Foucault is less likely to assert that 'all interpretations, or knowledge, are equally valid, or that there are not practical grounds for preferring one truth to another' (Olssen et al. 2004: 21). Epistemic relativism is more consonant with Foucault's work, which asserts, 'that all beliefs or knowledge are socially constructed, so that knowledge is contingent, neither the truth values nor criteria of rationality exist outside of historical time' (Olssen et al. 2004: 21). Subsequently, policy theorists might be seen as epistemic relativists for any claims about the status of policy, especially those invoked by the state, are always understood as contingent and contested.

The status of materiality is the locus of the second criticism of discursive approaches to power and policy. While materiality is significant for identifying the connections between education policy and the urban landscape, any understanding of these connections within and as a result of policy will always be discursive. Or as Olssen et al (2004) suggest, '[w]hile the material order thus maintains ... an autonomous ontological existence, in epistemological terms it is always mediated discursively' (p. 68). For example, there are obvious physical distinctions between areas where there has been policy-led investment, or gentrification, and disinvestment in the urban landscape. However, these distinctions represent different things for developers, home owners, people renting property, social housing residents, and the homeless. The discursive constitution of the landscape is as equally real as the steel beams and polished floorboards of warehouses converted into 'New-York style' lofts, or the broken windows and graffiti-covered walls of factories that are apparently abandoned. What remains significant is 'how language enters into the constitution of the world' (Hubbard 2006: 123).

The third criticism focuses on the apparently diminished role of the state in discursive conceptions of power and policy. This includes concern that what is lacking in 'micro-political' studies is a focus on state control over policy outcomes (e.g., Hatcher and Troyna 1994). Policy studies drawing on Foucault are certainly attentive to the role of the state; what differs from a critical theory approach is the conceptualisation of power, and thus how control, or otherwise, of policy outcomes might operate. In an interview relating to the disciplinary society and its links to the modern state, Foucault (1994d) clarifies that 'I don't want to say that the state isn't important' (p. 122). Nevertheless, his analytical focus is on relations of power proposed as beyond the limits of the state. This requires two assumptions: one, the state does not encompass, or pervade, all relations of power; and, two, the existence of the state requires other 'already-existing power relations' (pp. 122–123). Therefore, the determining role of the state in policy development and practice should be approached with caution, but not discarded.

As Ball (1994a, 1994b) argues, the state is not absent, rather it is reconceptualised in order to be attendant to how power/knowledges associated with policy are challenged and sustained in 'local' settings. Ball suggests:

> [p]olicies are always incomplete insofar as they relate to or map on to the 'wild profusion' of local practice. Policies are crude and simple. Practice is sophisticated, contingent, complex and unstable. (Ball 1994a: 10–11)

Critiques concerning the status of the state in discursive approaches to policy scholarship can also be framed in relation to notions of the macro and micro. Such critiques can be characterised as tensions between, and over, policy analyses focusing on the macro, with a concern about ideology and the state, and analyses examining the micro, with an interest in actors and practices (Simons et al. 2009b, Vidovich 2007). This tension within policy studies corresponds with what Peck and Tickell (2002) describe as 'walking the line' (p. 381) in studies of neoliberalism, a call for studies to be attendant to both specific, contingent 'local' instances of neoliberalism and the aspects of neoliberalism that connect places. Conceiving of the macro and micro as mutually constitutive underpins Deleuze and Guattari's (1987) contention that 'everything is political, but every politics is simultaneously a *macropolitics* and a *micropolitics*' (p. 213, original emphasis). To address this simultaneity, I turn to Foucault's 'governmental rationalities' which draw 'together the levels of "micro" and "macro" analyses of power' (Gordon 1994: xxv). In addressing this, I suggest these designations be put aside. As Miller and Rose (2008) note, governmentality can, at the least, evade the micro/ macro categorisation, and as such, 'avoid a simplistic and sequential style of analysis, notwithstanding the false sense of comfort it can induce' (p. 21).

GOVERNMENTALITY AND POLICY ANALYSIS

Studies of governmentality are traceable to a series of lectures and interviews given by Foucault, particularly his 1978 lectures on security, territory, and population. During his February 1 lecture Foucault suggests the 1978 lectures would be better titled 'a history of "governmentality"' (Foucault 2004: 108). He outlines three meanings of governmentality. One identifies the process of governmentalisation of the state, from a Middle Ages state of justice to an administrative state in the fifteenth and sixteenth centuries. Another meaning pertains to the ascendance of government as a form of power, linking governmental apparatuses to the development of specific forms, or 'series', of knowledge. The other interrelated meaning, and the one of most interest to me, posits governmentality as:

> the ensemble formed by institutions, procedures, analyses and reflections, calculations, and tactics that allow the exercise of this very specific, albeit very complex, power that has the population as its target, political economy as its major form of knowledge, and apparatuses of security as its essential technical instrument. (Foucault 2004: 108)

The central problematic of government as the conduct of conduct (Foucault 1994c), is the tension between the tendency towards state centralisation and the logics of dispersion, 'a problematic which poses questions of the *how* of government' (Peters 2009: xxx, original emphasis). In this book, I draw on what might be termed 'post-Foucauldian' notions of governmentality, developed by scholars such as Mitchell Dean (1999), Barry Hindess (Dean and Hindess 1998), Peter Miller and Nikolas Rose (2008). I am particularly interested in these scholars' examinations of government and governance in advanced liberal or neoliberal societies.

For me, the key points in the studies of neoliberal governmentality are: one, liberal government rationalities rely on agency constituted by legitimate knowledge and deployed through certain technologies (Dean and Hindess 1998); and two, power is conceptualised as dispersed, and consequently politics is conceived without reference to a coherent state as actor (Miller and Rose 2008). Significantly, this focus on a dispersed notion of power:

is not because states and the political apparatus are unimportant—that would be to misunderstand our argument. Rather, we argue that analyses should start from elsewhere, from the practices of governing themselves. (Miller and Rose 2008: 20)

The state continues to be significant in governmentality studies of public policy. I am interested in how the reconfiguring of the state both continues and disrupts its legitimating functions. While the contemporary state is governmentalised, it also continues as the nexus of political legitimacy, as 'the singularly accountable object in the field of political power' (Brown 2006: 83). As Brown argues, the governmentalised state is not only the manager of populations and producer of certain subjects. The state is also concerned with the reproduction of itself. The two functions cannot be separated. For Brown then:

> [t]his is not to say the state is the only source of governance, or even always the most important one; but where it is involved (and this includes privatization schemes in which the state's connection with the enterprises to which it turns over certain functions is still visible), the question of legitimacy is immediately at issue. (Brown 2006: 83)

What is intriguing to me is the dimension of legitimacy in public policy processes and practices. One specific aspect is how the conduct of individuals or collectives comes to be denoted as a public policy issue. That is, how issues are constituted and manifest in policy. To explore this I want to work broadly within ideas of rationalities and programmes of government, and technologies of government (Miller and Rose 2008). These conceptual distinctions are 'meant to indicate the intrinsic links between a way of representing and knowing a phenomenon, on the one hand, and a way of acting upon it so as to transform it' (Miller and Rose 2008: 15), yet also simultaneously be recognised as 'indissociable dimensions' (p. 16).

Policy and Generating Truths

Governmentality is not necessarily a theoretical framework or methodology *per se*, rather it can be a '*perspective* on governing and being governed' (Simons et al. 2009b: 67, original emphasis). One perspective could examine what is enabled, or the 'conditions of possibility', pertaining to policy texts, problems, solutions and actors (Simons et al. 2009b: 67). Orienting my policy analyses in this way 'implies that the very existence of a field of concerns termed "policy" should itself be treated as something to be explained' (Miller and Rose 2008: 28). In this conceptualisation of policy, it is possible, for example, to see how urban policy both reflects understandings of and constitutes the city (Cochrane 2007). As Osborne and Rose (1999) suggest, from the nineteenth century onwards, 'the government of the city becomes *inseparable from the continuous activity of generating truths about the city*' (p. 739, original emphasis).

In generating truths, policy is the frame of the problem which it ostensibly aims to solve. Policy problems, be they educational or urban, are not found outside of proposed policy solutions. Policy initiatives indeed both posit the problem and solutions or responses (Bacchi 2000). As Miller and Rose suggest, from the perspective of government, it is pointless to identify:

> a problem unless one simultaneously set[s] out some measures to rectify it. The solidity and separateness of 'problems' and 'solutions' are thus attenuated. Or, to put it differently, the activity of problematizing is intrinsically linked to devising ways to seek to remedy it. So, if a particular diagnosis or tool appears to fit a particular 'problem', this is because they have been made so they fit each other. (Miller and Rose 2008: 15)

This idea of policy as generating truths about the city and schooling can be illustrated through two examples. The first relates to area-based initiatives where state agencies coordinate to intervene in an area that is deemed to be statistically deprived. This statistical representation of deprivation becomes a truth about this area, notably that deprivation is measurable and solvable at the individual and area level. In the UK, education policy is a key part of area-based initiatives. Policy plays a role in either developing 'all-service schools' where social services are located on school grounds, or as part of extending schooling into the neighbourhood, outside the school gates so to speak (Power et al. 2005, Raffo and Dyson 2007). On the one hand, this seems to constitute the school as a site, or agent, of welfare first and foremost, a role deemed necessary before other educative roles can be undertaken. On the other hand, area-based initiatives in education may also focus explicitly on raising educational standards in urban areas of disadvantage, such as *Excellence in Cities* in the UK. Higher test scores are deemed to be necessary concomitant with addressing non-educational concerns, such as student diets and family financial planning. Education policy thus sanctions intervention at the level of the individual or family to address myriad concerns such as 'poor parenting', health problems, social 'dysfunction', and so forth.

A second related example of policy truths and the city pertains to the connections between gentrification, neoliberal urban policy, and the social mix (e.g., N. Smith 2002). As distinct from area-based initiatives where populations are to be remediated, the policy premise is a 'poor' or 'lack' of social mix, usually meaning few middle-class people, which it is argued results in urban areas of endemic disadvantage. There is a connection to area-based initiatives as the ideas of middle-class migration through gentrification, and a 'rebalancing' of social composition, are seen to connect with in-vogue policy concepts used in area-based initiatives, such as 'social capital'. However, rather than concentrate on directly remediating disadvantaged populations, policy initiatives promoting gentrification aim to break up what are seen as problematic concentrations of disadvantaged social groups.

Urban policy makers describe gentrification as 'urban regeneration', a term encapsulating an inclusive scope, and 'gentrification is thus recast as a positive and necessary environmental strategy' (Smith 2002: 445). Advocates for gentrification invoke the possibility of a socially mixed area and thus the potential beneficial outcomes for those disadvantaged populations who have not, as yet, been physically displaced. For advocates, such as Byrne (2003) in his paper "Two Cheers for Gentrification", creating a 'better' social mix:

> can ameliorate the social isolation of the poor. New more affluent residents will rub shoulders with poorer existing residents on the streets, in shops, and within local institutions, such as public schools. Such newcomers may exhibit possibilities of social mobility and a determination to secure adequate public services that provide existing residents with . . . role models. (Byrne 2003: 422)

This vision encompasses a newly formed diversity driven by middle-class in-migration whereby new residents foster 'community' and offer a hand-up for the 'socially excluded' (Lees 2008). However, as an example of how the social mix position is problematic, this overestimates both the agency of the 'newcomers' to effect neighbourhood social transformations (see Ley and Dobson 2008) and the willingness of those existing residents to accept being positioned as deficient to the 'incomers'.

Neoliberal Rationalities

I want to explore the political rationalities, programmes and technologies, of 'reflexive government' (Dean 1999), through the example of neoliberalism in relation to cities and education policy. Neoliberalism is often conflated with policy shifts based on five values: 'the individual; freedom of choice; market security; laissez faire, and minimal government' (Larner 2000: 7). These values then challenge the Keynesian welfare state by combining institutional economics, which includes public choice theory, with managerialism, and the ascendance of privatisation and deregulation. Neoliberalism is thus commonly equated with the decline or, perhaps more accurately, the rejection of the welfare state, and the ascendance of Chicago School economics, leading to the legitimacy of free trade and market competition as the organising principles of a global economy and policy enactments within and between nation states (Harvey 2005, Saul 2005). This assumes the key actors are politicians and bureaucrats, developing and implementing a coherent programme of converging policies as a response to problems of global capitalism (Larner 2000).

Cities are claimed to be the central objects and generators of neoliberal policy making, the primary sites of neoliberal manifestation, transpiration, and intensification (Brenner and Theodore 2002, Hackworth 2007). Aspects of these policy regimes include the state creation of urban development corporations and increased use of private public partnerships to achieve infrastructure goals, demarcating also a shift from ideas of social-democratic cities towards competitive cities as the model for urban policy. This shift means rethinking the role of the state in 'the reworking of inherited conceptions of citizenship, community and everyday life' (Brenner and Theodore 2005: 106).

It is thus important to recognise the political and philosophical rationalities underpinning these policies (Brown 2003, Larner 2000). Neoliberalism entails the very marketisation of the state (Dean 1999), with market rationality entering realms previously deemed 'either outside of or even antagonistic to the economic' (Burchell 1996: 27). Schooling and choice is such an example. While parental choice is one aspect of education markets, there is increasingly a concomitant emphasis on schools actively targeting the type of students they wish to attract. Schools that are well resourced and in high demand select desirable students, including modifying admission structures (Bowe et al. 1992, Olssen et al. 2004, Windle 2009). Schools unable to effectively market themselves end up in the residual position of educating 'unwanted' or 'unteachable' students (Youdell 2004). Additionally, this creation of residual schools perversely operates as a type of 'safety-net', which Campbell et al. (2009) suggest in Australia:

> is meant to 'catch' and provide some relief to citizens who for some reason of incapacity do not operate effectively within a market. Increasingly in education, especially in secondary education, it is the ordinary government comprehensive high schools that perform the safety net role. (Campbell et al. 2009: 5–6)

A lack of resources leads to, residual' schools providing fewer educational opportunities and facilities, and consequently, these schools are considered an inferior 'product'. Conflict arises between the educational aims of schools, and the market-driven requirements to attract 'successful' students (Marginson 1997b). I am interested in how policy constitutes a successful student or parent in an education market. I want to use this as a departure point to think about the way policies not only generate regimes of truth about schooling and the city, but also constitute 'ideal' urban and educational citizens.

Enabling Policy: Technologies and Steering at a Distance

Reflexive government is a system of thinking that is constitutive of the practices it addresses, operating through *technologies of government*. These technologies aim to produce various desirable and intelligible subjectivities.

As Burchell (1996) notes, for Foucault (1994a), government 'is a "contact point" where techniques of domination—or power—and *techniques of the self* "interact"' (p. 20, original emphasis). Constraining technologies of domination 'act upon the possibilities of action of other people. To govern in this sense is to structure the possible field of action of others' (Foucault 1994c: 341). Education policy supporting school choice provides a set of possibilities, a set of schooling options, perhaps previously absent from the repertoire of parental inclinations. These options include specialist schools, such as academically selective, sporting, or fine arts schools, in addition to an increasing number of private schools, which while beyond the remit of this book, also provide a range of low fee options for parents (Ball 2003, Campbell et al. 2009). These private schools, which in Australia and Canada are partially funded by either state or federal governments, usually provide schooling options on the basis of religion (e.g., Catholic, Islamic) or educational philosophies (e.g., Steiner schools).

Foucault's other contact point, 'technologies of the self', seems to offer possibilities of agency, as technologies:

> which permit individuals to effect by their own means or with the help of others a certain number of operations on their bodies and souls, thoughts, conduct, and way of being, so as to transform themselves in order to attain a certain state of happiness, purity, wisdom, perfection, or immortality. (Foucault 1988: 18)

The types of subjectivities enabled by these technologies of the self, encompassing the self-actualisation of the subject through what can be desired or dreamed of, are also constrained by what is an intelligible and an acceptable urban citizen, student, parent, and so forth (Bondi 2005, Davies and Petersen 2005, Youdell 2004). This interaction of technologies of domination and the self can be illustrated through reference to neoliberal education policy. Neoliberalism 'creates policies and practices that embody the enterprising and constantly strategizing entrepreneur out of the possessive individualism it establishes as the ideal citizen' (Apple 2001: 196). In a marketised educational policy environment what becomes intelligible is the reconfiguring of students, along with parents, as 'clients' (Kenway and Bullen 2001). Parents and students have the capacity to refashion themselves as educational entrepreneurs, diligently researching and evaluating the schooling options available *and* desired. However, at the same time as opportunity arises, such as increased capacity to choose schools or choose where to live, neoliberalism posits responsibility for success and failure as equivalent regardless of the constraints on these choices, such as educational background (Brown 2003).

These aspects of opportunity, responsibility, success, fear, desire, and failure are part of the rationalities, programmes, and technologies that enable the state to 'steer at a distance' (Rose 1996). This idea of steering has been utilized, or at the least inferred, in education policy studies, such as identifying the way policy works as 'non-interventionary intervention' (Ball 1998: 125), and references to policy in conjunction with a '"steering at a distance" modus operandi' (Lingard 2000: 48). This steering, or what Miller and Rose also call, 'government at a distance', is closely connected to various technologies (apparatuses, techniques, tools) that allow authorities (i.e., Ministries of Education, school districts, urban planners) to conceive of and then intervene to act upon the conduct of conduct, across varying proximities (Miller and Rose 2008). I am interested in the connections between political rationality and what occurs in places, including the focus on how particular policy discourses constitute specific desirable subjectivities, and how these are taken up, such as the constitution of citizen-consumers in education markets (the entrepreneurial principal, the choosing parent). As Marston and McDonald (2006) suggest, 'a governmental analytics invites researchers to think about individual subjects as being produced in specific social policy practices' (p. 3). Education policy is a useful way to examine these connections, for 'education policies take the form of political programmes of government and attempt to use technologies of government to implement these programmes in a way that is consistent with the underlying rationality of government' (Tikly 2003: 165–166). It should be noted that, education policy entails more than merely reflecting dominant rationalities, and it does not necessarily determine those subjectivities it enables.

A 'tricky theoretical problem': Rationalities and Indeterminate Outcomes

Critiques of governmental analyses are primarily focused on the production of, or the capacity to intervene to produce, subjectivity (e.g., Barnett et al. 2008). The locus of these critiques is that governmentality studies tend to overstate causality and intentionality. An example is how identifiable rationalities and programmes are translated, through technologies of government, into intentionally amenable and acceptable subjectivities, such as the active citizen, the meritorious student, and the citizen consumer.

Dean (1999) identifies this concern as the 'tricky theoretical problem' for governmentality studies. He asserts 'the problem of the disjunction between the explicit rationalities of government . . . and the more or less implicit logic of these practices' (p. 72), should be understood within the context of what is being proposed by governmentality studies. Dean contends:

> [t]he forms of identity promoted and presupposed by various practices and programmes of government should not be confused with a *real* subject, subjectivity or subject position, i.e. with a subject that is the endpoint or terminal of these practices and constituted through them. Regimes of government do not *determine* forms of subjectivity.

They elicit, promote, facilitate, foster and attribute various capacities, qualities and statuses to particular agents. They are successful to the extent that these agents come to experience themselves through such capacities (e.g. of rational decision making), qualities (e.g. as having a sexuality) and statuses (e.g. as being an active citizen). (Dean 1999: 32, original emphasis)

This idea of limits to determination seems clearly demonstrated in empirical studies of education markets which identify how some parents apparently refuse the designation of an entrepreneurial citizen. This includes parents who send their children to 'local' comprehensive, ethnically mixed schools. This decision is an amalgam of a complicated set of factors related to parents' conception of what is best for their children (e.g., Windle 2009). What this also seems to suggest is that in an education market all parents become vectors of policies when dealing with schools, where even the local school is a choice (Campbell et al. 2009). What differentiates these choices is individual parents' insistence on what educational practices pertain to and will benefit their child, and what practices do not. The parent in this sense is, like the student, also an educational subject.

For example, in the UK, Reay and colleagues (2008) identified the rationales and experiences of white, middle-class parents who choose to send their children to 'socially mixed, urban state schooling' in London and other UK urban centres. These parents seem to be the counter to the white, middle-class norm of self-interest represented through homogeneity, and, rather, are motivated by a desire for their children to mix with other children from a variety of class and especially ethnic backgrounds. However, these parents also consider it is to their children's advantage, socially and culturally, to attend these types of schools. These children obtain high academic results, at times much higher relative to other non-white or non-working-class students in these schools (Reay 2008, Reay et al. 2007). Even for these middle-class 'resisters' choice is predicated on merit either as the rewards of class or the responsibilities of class. What is enabled by policy and what is desired as an ideal urban, educational subject, thus makes ideas of resistance complex, for 'people are recruited into neoliberal forms of governmentality, even if they also, simultaneously, seek to resist some of its effects' (Bondi 2005: 499).

MOVING ON: GOVERNMENTALITY, ETHNOGRAPHY, AND SPACE

What is important for me in the critique of governmentality above is a methodological concern. This is the charge that too many governmental studies remain at the level of discursive analysis of texts (Marston and McDonald 2006). A discursive analysis of texts is a component of the examinations of policy initiatives throughout this book. However, this book also couples governmentality with ethnography as a way to examine practices in different places, to situate policy processes and practices, and 'to understand *how* policies are implemented, their effects in practice and attendant unforeseen circumstances' (Marston and McDonald 2006: 7, original emphasis). The affinities between approaches like genealogy, and governmentality, and ethnography, have been well rehearsed, notably focusing on context and interrogating regimes of power/knowledge (Tamboukou and Ball 2003). The grounding of this book in broadly ethnographic approaches is crucial to the investigation of neoliberal education policy and urban change, to being attendant to the practices of policy, and the examination of how and why specific subjectivities are constituted and taken up (Petersen 2009). And as will be evident it is important how and *where* these subjectivities are constituted and taken up.

On this last point, I am curious about the positioning of particular subjectivities and how 'technologies of government' operate spatially in the practices of educational policy change. I am interested in the ways policy provides conditions of possibility, or conditions of 'recruitment', for neoliberal educational subjectivities to be conceived and constituted. As such I want to look at how policy and subjectivity might be understood in relation to space and place. I therefore want to examine governmentality as spatial. As an aside, while I work from a critical policy studies stance in education, I think this spatial approach has some salience for policy studies more broadly, especially in urban studies where critical policy work is relatively underemphasised (Lees 2003).

As I noted in Chapter 1, educational policy and other policy analyses are increasingly drawing on spatial theories (Richardson and Jensen 2003, Thiem 2007). In the following chapter, I explore the possibilities for undertaking studies that move from merely seeing space as a context for policy to be made and unfold, to taking seriously the conceptual and empirical relationships between policy, subjectivity and space.

3 Notes on a Spatial Policy Analytic
Relational Notions of Subjectivity, Space, and Place

> Employed as a methodological approach, a constructivist spatial imaginary may . . . enhance emerging narratives of educational restructuring. Rather than context . . . or contingency, geography becomes both a stake and strategy in political mobilizations—a tool to initiate, stabilize, and contest policy change. (Thiem 2007: 32)

Ball (1994a) contends 'the *complexity* and *scope* of policy analysis . . . precludes the possibility of successful single-theory explanations. What we need in policy analysis is a toolbox of diverse concepts and theories' (p. 14, original emphasis). In this chapter I explicate how spatial theories are a useful, even necessary, part of critical policy analyses of inner city education markets. In tandem with Chapter 2, this chapter completes the conceptual terrain on which the forthcoming chapters are based.

I start this chapter by outlining concepts of subjectivity, to build on the discussion, in Chapter 2, on governmentality, and the constitution of desirable, and undesirable, subjectivities. I cover salient understandings of, and connections between, race[1] and class to be applied and rethought throughout the book. I begin to show how space and subjectivity are mutually constitutive, a prelude to my explication of space and place in the latter part of the chapter. I then move to identify reasons for the 'spatial turn' in the social sciences, including education. I conclude the chapter by specifying, and illustrating, relational ideas of space and place, premised on notions of interrelations, multiplicity, and openness.

A BRIEF EXEGESIS ON RACE AND THE MIDDLE CLASSES

A series of interconnecting terms appear in the following chapters, notably, 'identity', the 'subject', and 'subjectivity'. I use identity when this term is also used by cited authors; however, in general, I use subjectivity. I prefer this term for, at least in educational research, identity continues to carry with it an association with the individual as a coherent, rational, knowing subject. Conversely, I want to work with the idea of the socially constructed subject, broadly conceived.

In this book I am primarily interested in how race and class are made meaningful in relation to each other, particularly the intelligibility of social categories and certain types of desirable and recognisable subjects (e.g., Petersen and O'Flynn 2007). This is related to performativity, and the role of discourse and discursive practices in producing that which it names (Butler 1993). Youdell (2006) notes that for Butler this means 'the subject must be performatively constituted in order to make sense *as* a subject' (p. 43, original emphasis), and must be 'recognisable in the discourses that are circulating in the settings and moments in which they are deployed' (p. 44).

I want to engage with the idea that it is not only the middle classes, but specifically the white middle classes, that are the privileged norm (Reay 2008), or more precisely the intelligible subject in education policy in Sydney, London, and Vancouver. Somewhat contradistinctively, I briefly deal separately with the categories of class, race, and whiteness.

A Note on the Middle Classes

Recent work on class has arguably been less interested in socio-economic classification, labour market positions or production, and more with identity (Dowling 2009). My interest lies with this emphasis, while recognising that class analysis retains saliency depending upon the question or issue under investigation (Wright 2005). For my purposes, I am most concerned with how available discourses of the middle classes constitute and are drawn upon in the processes and practices of neoliberal education policy in urban settings.

I am interested in the middle class for two reasons. The first relates to education policy and the claimed centrality of middle-class interests. That is, contemporary education policy is primarily aimed at accommodating, and constituting, the interests of the middle class. This leads to class advantage in education, with the middle class active and successful in creating this accommodation and convergence of interests (Ball 2003, Reay 2008). The second reason I focus on the middle class pertains to urban policy and the transformation of urban spaces. This is to be cognisant of the ways 'elements of processes of class colonization and residence, remain key to geographical thinking' (Dowling 2009: 835). This is particularly the case in relation to urban transformations such as gentrification, which can be considered part of a middle-class remaking of the inner city (Butler and Robson 2003, Ley 1996). Overall, I am concentrating on *how* the middle classes are discursively constituted in schooling and in the city, and the role of policy in the enabling and valorising of middle-class practices (Gewirtz 2001).

Race and Whiteness

A wide variety of research has dealt with the ways education markets produce racialisations and racism (e.g., Apple 2001, Levine-Rasky 2008,

Youdell 2004). Other work has connected education markets, race, and urban change. This includes Lipman's (2007) study on Chicago, which examines the connections between neoliberal policy processes and practices and the closure of inner city schools. The closed schools had a high proportion of students of colour while other schools, servicing mainly white students, remained open. Relatedly, in this book I focus on the ways schools and areas of the city are given racial meaning, and importantly how this racial meaning is mobilised in education policy processes and practices.

It will become apparent that in this book, for the most part, I do not use the word ethnicity, despite the cities under investigation being possibly construed as multicultural cities. In one sense, ethnicity can be deployed as a way of representing the possibilities for cultural transformation: ethnicity as acceptable difference (Jenkins 2003). In another sense, ethnicity is often used interchangeably with race in social science research.

I explicitly use the term race to explore a prevalent perniciousness in relation to issues of power and policy in the inner city (Keith and Cross 1993). I remain cognisant of how using race even as an analytical category reinforces its significance (Keith 2005); more pointedly, I am aware that race as a concept is perhaps beyond recuperation (Gilroy 2000). Nevertheless, I am choosing to keep race in play, for I want to explore how the geographies of education policy operate to produce race. This is also to work from the position that race always carries with it an implicit connection to the explicit enactment of racism. When:

> invoked to mark the human, race almost invariably operates as *threat*, as pernicious, as disruptive. Racism, of course, always incorporates race within it as basis of conceptual differentiation. In that sense, racisms can be said to order race, to require and to fabricate it. But the related point I am pushing here . . . is the complementary one, at once simpler and more obscure. Race, in short, is never far from racism. (Goldberg 2009: 355, original emphasis)

In looking at the idea that race is never far from racism in relation to policy, I am conceptualising race as neither wholly socially constructed or essentialised, especially through biology (for overview see Nayak 2006). I am interested in race as a category that is kept in play as 'the *product* of prevailing discourses (regimes of truth) that *make* race and ethnicity *as if* they were biologically or culturally fixed' (Gillborn and Youdell 2009: 180–181, original emphasis). This discursive approach focuses on how racial meaning is constituted and foregrounds the power relations that make race and racism a contingent accomplishment (Nayak 2004, 2006).

I take this discursive approach to also work with the ideas of whiteness. As a social concept, whiteness is distinct from white people, although the presence of white bodies often conflates the two (Leonardo 2009). It is thus important to identify 'whiteness . . . [as] a racial perspective or a world-view'

(Leonardo 2002: 31) that posits racial meaning as essentialist and non-relational, and which allows its operation, the operation of whiteness, to be denied (Dwyer and Jones 2000). This can be illustrated in reference to urban Aboriginality, and contestation over what is and is not an acceptable role for Aboriginal people in schooling and the inner city. Aboriginal students in inner city education markets can be marked as dangerous and undesirable students by white parents who mobilise discourses of the racial 'other', whilst denying their own racialisation, and rejecting their actions as racist.

Furthermore, what this example indicates is how subjectivities have constitutive relationships with space and place (Longhurst 2003, Probyn 2003). This includes how spatial legitimacy is conferred, how ideas of belonging are defined, and the role proximity and difference play in the constitution of subjectivities.

SPACE NOW: ON THE SPATIAL (RE)TURN
IN THE SOCIAL SCIENCES

> The great obsession of the nineteenth century was, as we know, history: with its themes of development and of suspension, of crisis and cycle, themes of the ever-accumulating past, with its great preponderance of dead men and the menacing glaciations of the world. . . . The present epoch will perhaps be above all the epoch of space. We are in the epoch of simultaneity; we are in the epoch of juxtaposition, the epoch of the near and far, of the side-by-side, of the dispersed. (Foucault 1986: 22)

The above, much cited passage appears so provocative and so dismissive of time that it must either be affirmed or rejected. Yet Foucault is not necessarily antagonistic toward time (for discussion see Soja 1996). This would be somewhat absurd considering Foucault's application of archaeology and genealogy. What is rarely cited is that Foucault (1986) continues, 'it is not possible to disregard the fatal intersection of time with space' (p. 22), an acknowledgement of the inseparability of space and time that is now well established (see Massey 1993a).

What Foucault seems to be describing are the characteristics of spatialities that came to the fore in the twentieth century. However, arguably, there was not a parallel spatial ascension in the social sciences that was sustained and coherent. This incoherence meant that despite being the epoch of space, in the twentieth century spatial analyses continued to be underrepresented in the social sciences in deference to historical analysis (see Soja 1996). Nonetheless, it is possible to trace spatial approaches across a range of disciplines and fields, including linguistics, and a revitalisation of spatial disciplines such as geography (see Peters and Kessl 2009). Moreover, Warf and Arias (2009) suggest there was a distinct spatial turn in the social sciences in latter parts of the twentieth century. This turn was predicated on the idea that '[g]eography matters, not for the simplistic and overly used reason that everything happens in space, but because *where* things happen is critical to knowing *how* and *why* they happen' (Warf and Arias 2009: 1, original emphasis).

It now appears common sense to recognise the spatialisation of contemporary life, and the multiple forms of communication networks and modes of mobility increasingly connecting and disconnecting individuals across the planet. Yet, in recognising this spatial turn, it is also necessary, at least to my mind, to acknowledge and engage with Neil Smith's point that:

> [t]here is a crucial question of the extent to which this 'spatial turn' has been more than skin deep. . . . Put most crudely, perhaps, why space? Why *should* our analysis of social difference and political possibility be rewritten in the language of space? (Smith 2004: 13, original emphasis)

One response to 'why space?' is framed by disciplinary and interdisciplinary concerns. The spatial turn conceivably reflects recent directions in social theory closely linked to those in postmodern and feminist theory (e.g., Gupta and Ferguson 1997, Soja 1989). Crang and Thrift (2000) suggest 'the role of space in the construction of theory is itself important, not only in the ways that theory might apply to a spatially distributed world, but in the spatialities that allow thought to develop particular effectivities and intensities' (p. 3). Spatial ideas can be used to try and think differently about education policy in inner city areas; as both an affirmation of the obvious, such as school choice policies operating to spatially re-order students between schools; and an unsettling of the familiar, such as reconsidering enduring macro/micro distinctions in educational policy analysis. This includes thinking spatially about how governmental rationalities translate into the take-up of desired subjectivities. As Allen notes (2003, 2004), the 'micro' aspects of governmentality are explicitly identified in analyses of such things as prisons and schools. However, Allen suggests there is somewhat less detail on the 'macro' operations of a dispersed notion of power. Similarly, Murdoch (2006) points to the 'need to attend to the precise mechanisms that allow spatially dispersed and seemingly autonomous and independent subjects to be aligned with particular strategies of discipline and normalization' (pp. 52–53).

A second response to 'why space?' and to also perhaps 'why space now?', is to posit the spatial turn as more than an academic pursuit and to denote it as being closely related to Foucault's concerns above; that is, related to contemporary transformations in economies, politics, and culture. This view 'asserts that we cannot comprehend the production of spatial ideas independent of the production of spatiality' (Warf and Arias 2009: 5). Contemporary transformations associated with the production of spatiality include globalisation (with all its attendant ambiguities and ambivalences), cyberspace, immigration, and environmental challenges, including climate change (Warf and Arias 2009).

In the educational arena the spatial transformation of schooling through the introduction and consolidation of markets has contributed to the development of, and contestation over, methodologies. There have been significant debates concerning whether education markets should be examined at a systemic level or local level (Gibson and Asthana 2000, Gorard and Fitz 1998). In some sense this is a result of differing foci. Much school choice work has focused on the processes of choice rather than the outcomes, with resulting contention over whether or not education markets have lead to systemic segregation (Taylor 2009a). Therefore, it appears the geographies of school choice need to be examined in a sustained and sophisticated manner. As Taylor notes:

> [a]lthough space and place are often central to many sociological studies of school choice, there have been few attempts to describe and consolidate the main geographical characteristics of school choice— reflecting the uneven spaces of choice and competition in any given urban market. The focus in many studies tends to be on how space constrains choice rather than the way space and choice interrelate. (Taylor 2009a: 552)

This absence of space as concept, rather than merely context, reflects problems across the social sciences. While space is becoming increasingly important to critical endeavours in the social sciences, eliding conceptualisations of space nonetheless continues to neglect and perpetuate 'the problematic nature of spatiality' (Keith and Pile 1993: 223). This neglect is in part due to disagreements over the definitional parameters of space across disciplines, from physics to philosophy (see Nerlich 1994). Crang and Thrift (2000) also suggest the 'problem is not so much that space means very different things—what concepts do not—but that it is used with such abandon that its meanings run into each other before they have been properly interrogated' (p. 1). In attempting to address this problem I want to outline and employ a particular idea of 'social' space.

SOCIAL SPACE(S)

> Just as none of us is outside or beyond geography, none of us is completely free from the struggle over geography. (Said 1993: 7)

In the following sections I highlight some understandings of space that are later mobilised and deployed in the following chapters. While I accord primacy to certain approaches, I do not assume that one approach to space serves all purposes, for 'there is no one kind of space' (Thrift 2006: 141). For example, spaces of schooling could be considered in light of the idea of absolute space which is independent of entities and characterised as a container (see Hubbard et al. 2004). This would designate schools as spaces in waiting, always already, to be filled by students, teachers, and so forth, but bearing no constitutive power on the relations occurring in these schools.

What I am talking about in this book can be broadly conceived as 'social space'. The idea of social spaces is central to Henri Lefebvre's book, *The Production of Space*, (1991) which outlines a dialectical relationship between the production of (social) space and the production of social relations. Farrar (1997) criticises this relationship, arguing 'socially produced space' is a circular construction consisting of space producing that which produces it. There is no sociological understanding of how social processes unfold and no sense of human action, and too much emphasis on space and spatiality as ill-defined structure.

Despite this critique, I am convinced that understanding the processes and practices of educational policy in inner city locations requires a general orientation to social space that 'move[s] away from the Kantian perspective on space—as an absolute category—towards *space as process* and *in process* (that is space and time combined in becoming)' (Crang and Thrift 2000: 3, original emphasis). The idea of space as becoming corresponds with the idea of subjectivity and policy as provisional, and allows the possibility of thinking differently about education policy in the city. Specifically it permits a focus on what policy spaces are made possible, and what are deferred or subjugated, and about how this occurs as a spatial politics.

Topologies Rather than Topographies: On the Invocation of Relational Space

This book works from and with relational notions of space, that are partly associated with poststructural geographies (Murdoch 2006). Jones (2009) contends 'the spatial project for relational thinkers is to replace topography and structure-agency dichotomies with a topological theory of space, place and politics as encountered, performed, and fluid' (p. 492). For my purposes, the relational approach to space can perhaps go some way to trying to understand the seeming absence of space, other than metaphorical, in studies of governmentality (Allen 2003, Argent 2005). On the basis of this promise I want to explicate three aspects of the relational spatial project pertaining to interrelations, multiplicity, and openness (Massey 2005).

The first aspect of a relational view is that space is produced through interrelations of identities/entities, premised on a refusal to accede a determining structure to space. As Murdoch (2006) asserts, 'spaces are made of complex sets of relations so that any spatial "solidity" must be seen as an accomplishment, something that has to be achieved in the face of flux and instability' (p. 23). This requires a commitment to the unsettling idea of entities and identities (or subjectivities) as contingent and provisional. Policy operates as one mode of provisional spatial ordering, that paradoxically can perhaps be construed as a spatial relations of provisional permanence (Jones 2009). This includes the introduction of area-based initiatives through a process by which one or more governmental agencies identify 'problem' areas, usually on the basis of indices of deprivation, and create bounded areas of policy intervention. More generally, educational and urban policy retains and requires spatial relations of permanence to be intelligible. Dikeç (2007) notes in reference to governmental practices that they 'are not merely "confined" to designated spaces. They constitute those spaces as part of the governing activity' (p. 280).

The second part of the relational project is to take stock of multiplicity, to recognise plurality as a necessary condition of relational space. This is to see space as the realm of concurrent, distinct, heterogeneity (Massey 2005). What characterises this approach in reference to the study of the city is:

> a strong emphasis on understanding cities as spatially open and cross-cut by many different kinds of mobilities, from flows of people to commodities and information. . . . This is not just a simple statement of multiplicity, but a recognition that urban life is the irreducible product of mixture. (Amin and Thrift 2002: 3)

It is interesting to me to think about mixture and student mobility, or more literally travel. Students travel all over cities as they move between residences and schools, often as a result of market-orientated policies that allow students to attend schools distant from their homes (see Symes 2007a). There is also a city-specific nature to this mobility. For example, travel for students in London may be different from Sydney, which has a long history of private schooling and student travel (see Symes 2007b). The specific modes of travel also differ, whether by bus, by foot, by car, by bicycle, or by train. Mobility as a component of markets illustrates that 'the boundaries of educational life are limitless ones, which extend beyond the compass of the school' (Symes 2007a: 443). As students travel, they constitute the city and different parts of the city in multiple ways, the city as dangerous, vibrant, gentrified, multicultural, home, strange, familiar, and so forth. Student travel is about encounters with multiplicity.

Urry (2003) notes '"[m]eetingness", and thus different forms and modes of travel, are central to much social life, a life involving strange combinations of increasing distance and intermittent co-presence' (p. 156). 'Meetingness' seems implicit in Sennett's conception of active edges, which in urban planning translates as 'a febrile zone of interaction and exchange, a zone where differences are activated' (Sennett 1999: 23). School students travelling across cities, congregating at transport hubs, shopping centres, parks, and so forth, are possible education market manifestations of the active edge. However, these 'febrile zones' need to be qualified. Symes (2007a) outlines how train travel to school in Sydney, by students attending private and public schools, creates spaces of interaction. These 'performances of travel' on station platforms and in railway carriages, are forms of bringing together students outside of school boundaries. Yet Symes also notes that the separation between private and public schooling remains even in these performance spaces; the marketised active edge is possibility not predetermination.

Relational space as multiplicity also depends on the contingency of proximity and distance (Allen 2004). Proximity and distance are not only about measurement, for 'distance—like difference—is not an absolute, fixed and given, but is set in motion and made meaningful through cultural practices' (Gregory 2004: 18). This idea provides a spatial understanding of the purported demise of the 'local neighbourhood school' in education markets. The design of catchment areas, which denoted the 'local school', was intended to represent the idea of locality and community. Ideally all children would attend neighbourhood elementary and comprehensive secondary schools (Vinson 2002). Additionally:

> [t]he cogency of the comprehensive ideal, which, even in the context of neoliberal policies still has many proponents, is one underpinned with the idea that placement of schools ought not to be taken lightly for it can promote social cohesion. (Symes 2007b: 175)

However, in an education market attending the 'local' school, even if this is closest to where a student lives, becomes enmeshed in the cultural politics and practices of school choice, where fear and uncertainty about whether a school is good enough becomes a paramount concern, intertwined with the circulation of school reputations (Ball 2003). Campbell et al. (2009) suggest that prior to the rise of education markets it was the choice of the non-local school that needed to be justified, usually on the grounds of religion, class affiliation, or family tradition. Conversely, now the choice of the local school needs to be justified. While '"[l]ocal" remains a virtue for most middle-class parents . . . "local" has also become synonymous for a large number of schools that are "not quite good enough"' (Campbell et al. 2009: 135).

The third aspect of relational space pertains to the idea of openness, as the entry point for politics. Space as interactional emphasises there are connections that have both been made and are yet to be made, and some that may never be accomplished. Space as product of these relations depends on multiplicity.

> However, these are not the relations of a coherent, closed system within which, as they say, everything is (already) related to everything else. Space can never be that completed simultaneity in which all interconnections have been established and in which everywhere is already linked with everywhere else. A space, then, which is neither a container

for always-already constituted identities nor a completed future of ho-
lism. (Massey 2005: 11–12)

Thus, this is not unfettered openness, for, '[w]hile constructed, space is
not infinitely malleable' (Thiem 2007: 32). This necessitates examining how power is mediated at different times and in different spaces; an
identification of the difference geography makes in understanding power
(Allen 2003, 2004). This can mean thinking about how educational market polices provide particular ways of shaping the role of schooling in the
city. Policy reconfigures the spatialities of residence and school by giving
primacy to choice, as illustrated by the above example of decline of the
geography of the local, of place, as the primary factor in deciding which
school to attend.

SPACE AND PLACE: DISTINCTION NOT DISJUNCTURE

Space and place have often been conflated, with Creswell (2004) suggesting
social space (following Lefebvre 1991) is for the most part indivisible from
the idea of place. Etymologically, the distinction is often made by English-
speaking theorists. As Shields notes, scholars who work in languages other
than English:

> have felt at ease with the use of the full range of meanings, denota-
> tive and connotative, of '*spazio*' and '*l'espace*'. In the *Dictionnaire
> Larousse, 'l'espace'* denotes 'place' (*lieu*), 'site' or an area, 'surface', or
> 'region'. '*L'espace*' does not mean just 'space'. (Shields 2006: 147)

Alternatively, place is often positioned in a binary with space: place *or*
space, place *over* space, space *over* place (for an elegantly concise discussion of the place/space binary see Agnew 2005).

These binaries of space and place have been connected to ideas of the
global and the local. One way of understanding this has been to attribute
authenticity and the unfolding of everyday life to place and the local, while
the global is deemed to be the space of abstract flows (of capital, of people,
etc.). However, it is somewhat problematic to conflate a fixed local with
everyday life for the boundaries of everyday life are not readily discerned,
they are tied into the transnationality of urban experiences (Smith 2001).
A related argument is the global, as the realm of dynamism, produces
change in the local, which can therefore only ever be about resistance
(Massey 1994b, 2005, 2007). Alternatively, the global and local can be
seen as 'discursively and practically constructed "positionalities" that [are]
appropriated and deployed by specific social forces at particular times'
(Smith 2001: 2). This provides a way of conceptualising education markets
so as to recognise the manifestation of a global neoliberal policy realm

(Forsey et al. 2008), while also acknowledging that education markets are necessarily realised in places (Taylor 2002, 2010).

This is to see place as part of wider socio-spatial relations (Massey 1993b). It also emphasises process, and ideas of encounter, difference, and negotiation. Places become *'moments of encounter,* not so much as "presents", fixed in time and space, but as variable events; twists and fluxes of interrelation' (Amin and Thrift 2002: 30, original emphasis). Places as events (see also Massey 2005) is to see places as temporary achievements that 'are no more and no less than moments of arbitrary closure. Materially produced and multiply signified, "a place" in precise terms can have only a meaning of a particular moment' (Keith 2005: 75). Additionally, the notion of events provides an interesting impetus to thinking about multiplicity and relational notions of place(s). In Sydney and Vancouver catchment areas are legacies of policy environs enacted prior to the dominance of choice policies. These boundaries are made sense of by parents in decisions about where to live and where to send their children to school. Catchment areas are spatially salient as boundaries to be utilised as a market guarantee or undercut as part of a market threat.

Catchment areas, prior to the introduction of ostensibly open enrolment policies, have long been a determinant of where parents with the capacity to do so, choose to live. In Australia, the UK, and North America, choice of residence for the middle classes has been closely related to the strength of schools, with resultant 'post-code segregation' (DeSena 2006, Robson and Butler 2001). Every real estate sign in front of a house with a 'good' school nearby is sure to point out that the house is in the right catchment area. A catchment area is thus utilised as a guarantee that your child will be accepted into a desired public school. For it is only by being in a catchment area that one can actually subvert the operations of the education quasi-market in which a school is able to select and turn away students who are outside of a catchment area.

This is open enrolment as representing both the possibility and threat of the market. While parents are able to choose to send their children to any government school, there are no guarantees of entry. Boundaries that are apparently open are quickly closed as the catchment area continues to be the guarantee. This reconfigures and distorts attachments to place as residence, in which parents and students can become simulacra of residents. Parents attempt to invoke the catchment guarantee by pretending that their children live in catchment areas when they primarily live elsewhere. This means '[p]roperties are rented for a time, and the within-zone residential addresses of relatives are used in the enrolment paperwork' (Campbell et al. 2009: 127).

Place as an event also brings together the aspects of relational space, interrelations, multiplicity, and openness, in reference to the 'thrown-togetherness, the unavoidable challenge of negotiating a here-and-now' (Massey 2005: 140). This challenge can be illustrated through reference to social mixing, and the benefits of mixed communities, urban change, and education. The most pervasive assumption underpinning neighbourhood renewal programmes and their relation to education is that increasing the residential social mix in inner urban areas under stress will result in more socially mixed schools (for critique see Lupton and Tunstall 2008). In a study of Chicago, Lipman (2008) outlines the connections between education and neoliberal urban change, involving '[d]owntown living and gentrified neighbourhoods, as well as new "innovative" schools in gentrified communities and choice within the public school system' (p. 121). Advocates promote mixed income schools as a desirable policy initiative on the premise that white, middle-class students and parents will become role models for low-income students, especially Black and Latino/a students. Lipman concludes that 'the discourse of mixed-income housing and schools reframes the reality of disinvestment, displacement subsidies to developers, and racial exclusion as opportunity for low-income people of colour' (p. 128). What is evident is how policy enables certain possibilities of place, policy underscores a negotiation of throwntogetherness. The premise of mixed income schools on the basis of providing role models denies the possibly of other negotiations between those parents and students deemed role models and those who are deemed deficient and in need.

AN ORIENTATION TO A SPATIAL POLICY ANALYTIC

The purpose of this chapter has been to illustrate the possibilities of, indeed an orientation in, policy studies of inner city schooling towards what might be termed a spatial policy analytic. This orientation posits subjectivity as co-constitutive with spatiality, to see subjectivity as historically and geographically contingent. An adherence to openness and multiplicity in issues of identity is to also posit these as significant when it comes to understanding space—it is to adhere to a relational approach to space and place. Space is thus invoked as more than context in educational policy studies, rather a critical policy analysis employing ideas of relational space and place is an analysis trying to recognise and articulate how power is manifested in, and by, spaces and places. It is an attempt to understand the difference that geography makes in identifying the dispersed and provisional nature of power. It is to take seriously the spatial aspects of governmental rationalities, programmes, and technologies.

However, I want to be clear that what I have outlined in this chapter is not meant to preclude other ways of constructing such a spatial analytic (e.g., Richardson and Jensen 2003, Thomson 2007, Taylor 2007). Rather what I have outlined is an attempt to develop some sense of the possible conceptual resources necessary to understand the complexity of education policy and the city. It is these resources that I bring to bear in the following chapters on Sydney, London and Vancouver.

4 Aboriginality, Racialised Places, and the Education Market in Inner Sydney

Population growth in the inner city has been strong in recent years. Some claim that this means there will be an increased future demand for school places. . . . The evidence does not, however, support this. This is because the character of the growth in the inner city population is such that it produces a comparatively low proportion of school age children. (New South Wales Department of Education and Training 2001b: 6)

In 2001 the New South Wales Department of Education and Training (DET) released a policy document, *Building the Future: An Education Plan for Inner Sydney (Draft Proposal)* (DET 2001a) which proposed restructuring inner city public schooling, in the form of closures and amalgamations of more than fifteen primary and secondary schools across inner Sydney. The policy process included the initial draft plan, a ten-week consultation period from March to May 2001, and the subsequent release of *Building the Future: Consultation Report* (DET 2001b). Rationales for structural change included market-based issues such as declining student numbers, curriculum narrowing, and increased demand for academically selective secondary school places. A discourse of recursive market decline was posited, in which 'families see the falling numbers at some local schools and choose to send children elsewhere for a sense of confidence and stability' (DET 2001a: 4). Additionally, the *Building the Future* proposal recognised 'the importance of locality—the social geography of schooling' (Blackmore 2002: 38), with the DET arguing, for instance, that families are 'moving from inner city to outer suburban areas for affordable housing' (DET 2001a: 4). This is a particular view of the city that precludes some families. Not all families, such as those in social housing, are capable of making decisions to move residences, even if another area is deemed more affordable.[1] That aside, the *Building the Future* policy documents presented a model for the 'revitalisation' of inner city schooling that was inexorably connected to the changing inner city.

This chapter explores the complex connections between Aboriginality, place, and schooling in reference to *Building the Future*. I focus on the policy processes and practices associated with Redfern, Waterloo, and Alexandria Primary Schools and Cleveland Street High School. These schools were closed and amalgamated to become Alexandria Park Community

School, opening in 2003. In this chapter I first examine how the DET mobilised demographics to justify the restructuring of inner city schooling. I then move to an extended discussion of the problematic status of Aboriginality in the inner city and in inner city schooling. I explore the ways policy discourses associated with Alexandria Park Community School position gentrification as a positive aspect of urban change. Gentrification is racialised and is deemed to import new 'non-Aboriginal' students to the inner city (the white middle classes), who, if attracted to the school, will constitute an ostensibly favourable repositioning of the school in an education market. I focus on the practices associated with this repositioned market to understand how this potentially reconstitutes Aboriginal students as entrepreneurial subjects.

CONTESTING POLICY AND THE MOBILISATION OF SPACE

During late 2001 and early 2002, school and community-based groups actively lobbied to make changes to the *Building the Future* programme, hoping to prevent the closure of a number of schools. The New South Wales (NSW) Labor government faced an upcoming election in 2003, and after sustained political pressure, the opposition parties in the NSW Parliament's Upper House struck the *Inquiry into proposed closure and restructuring of inner Sydney schools*. This inquiry, held under the aegis of the New South Wales Parliament Legislative Council: General Purpose Standing Committee No 1 (Legislative Council), included a series of public proceedings during May and June 2002.[2] The transcripts of the inquiry illustrate significant disagreements between individuals and groups over the directions set out in the *Building the Future* policy documents. Many submissions to the inquiry alluded to the range of inner city 'community' uses for the schools threatened with closure. What I examine is how these disagreements highlight the DET's designation of spatial knowledges as legitimate and illegitimate in the *Building the Future* policy process.

The DET constructed a sense of inevitability about closing inner city schools through recourse to enrolment data and demographics of the inner city. The school data showed that over the course of twenty years enrolments in the inner city had fallen, in some cases by over 40 percent. A key reason given for declining enrolments in the inner city was a significant shift from government schools to non-government secondary schools (Legislative Council 2002c: 4), reflecting a wider trend in Australian education (Campbell et al. 2009). Additionally, the DET argued falling enrolments were attributable to changes in inner city demographics, and the dominant group in the inner city was, or would become, childless professionals; yuppies and DINKs would not be the right kind of population to sustain inner city public schooling.

Those opposed to school closures also mobilised demographics to identify errors in the DET's conclusions. For example, Erskineville Primary School was slated to close and the DET maintained this was due to declining enrolment numbers and an unfavourable demographic outlook, including fewer children in this part of the inner city. Ms Mulvey, the president of the Erskineville Primary School Parents and Citizens Association (P & C) asserted that:

> [t]he [DET's] case for closure of Erskineville Public School rests on decline of enrolments and outdated ABS data. They focus on the past. The Erskineville Parents and Citizens Association case that we have documented many times to [the DET] rests on the most current demographics. (Legislative Council 2002d: 2)

This debate about future enrolments became one about accuracy. However, what remained unchallenged is the status of demographics as legitimate, 'scientific' knowledge (Petersen 2004) about the city and schooling. There are further examples scattered throughout the Inquiry transcripts that invoke and depend on demographic knowledge. Demographers brought in to support and refute the DET's claims made statements such as:

> Therefore . . . the second [demographic] report . . . I have to say I think that it is slighted a bit favourably towards Hunters Hill High School, *but it is a scientific piece of work* . . . The other [demographic] reports by Yusuf et al, and also by Phibbs, are *scientific pieces of work*. (Legislative Council 2002c: 41, my emphasis)

> I think, given a number of the assumptions, that both sets of [demographic] reports are fair. *They are both scientific inquiries.* (Legislative Council 2002c: 42, my emphasis)

However, during the Inquiry, Dr Phibbs, a demographer from the University of Sydney, challenged the possibility of accurately forecasting future enrolments. After reading the DET demographic report used to justify closing schools such as Erskineville he stated that:

> [w]hen I read it I was a little alarmed because I think it gave the impression that forecasting is a more precise science than it actually is. I cannot remember the last time I saw a forecast that was correct. There are so many risks involved in forecasting that basically a better way to think of them is as estimates. (Legislative Council 2002d: 6)

Demographic reports used in a contested policy process like *Building the Future* can be challenged in terms of the claims made, and even in terms of the predictive function of the demographic forecasting, that is whether they can actually be predictive of future trends. However, the epistemological underpinning of these claims is unquestioned.

The significance of statistical approaches like demography is apparent when considered as part of the technologies of government. Demography, as used in the case of the *Building the Future* reforms, represents the inner city and schooling in an accessible form for policy intervention. The complexity and multiplicity of the inner city and the contested terrain of schooling is inscribed as stable, and subsequently diagnosable, in this policy representation. Statistics render reality:

> in a form in which it can be debated and diagnosed. Information in this sense is not the outcome of a neutral recording function. It is itself a way of acting upon the real, a way of devising techniques for inscribing it in such a way as to make the domain in question susceptible to evaluation, calculation, and intervention. (Miller and Rose 2008: 65–66)

I want to be clear that I am not accusing the field of demography, or statistical analysis more broadly, of being illegitimate inquiries into the nature of reality. Rather I aim to highlight the political use of demography as one way of representing the city and schooling. The use of statistics in *Building the Future* reflects a broader characterisation. That is, '[n]umbers carry a special kind of influence in contemporary policy debates, where statistics are generally equated with scientific rigour and objectivity' (Gillborn 2010a: 270). Numbers have a force in policy rhetoric, often greater than words. Statistics are apportioned a level of legitimacy, a level of truth, denied to other forms of understanding the city and schooling.

For the DET, the inner city and the inner city schools were, 'absolute' or 'empty spaces' (Hubbard et al. 2004), waiting to be filled with residents, workers and students. Conversely, relational forms of spatial understanding were mobilised in the inquiry, including references to the significance of urban Aboriginality as a reason for preventing the closure of Redfern Primary. Ms Munroe, the Aboriginal chairperson of Redfern Primary School P & C, stated:

> Thank you for the opportunity to speak today. I would like to begin by acknowledging that the land we stand on today is Kuttabul land. I think by making that acknowledgement I come to you with a whole different aspect about history and learning and teaching, Aboriginal history, our sense of place. We have a very strong affinity with the Redfern community; we have a very long, proud association with the Redfern school, . . .
>
> A sense of place. . . . Redfern Primary School has it, a sense of place, a sense of history, a sense of pride . . . I can go to Redfern Primary School and point out the history of Gough Whitlam and Vincent Lingarie [and

the struggle for land rights[3]]. I cannot do that in any other school in that local area. I can go to that school and talk about whose land it is, and all the other pieces of Aboriginal land in the close vicinity to Redfern School. . . . That aspect of history is being forgotten in this whole process, our contribution of Aboriginal people to the Redfern community and to the Redfern area in particular, and our strong association with that school. (Legislative Council 2002d: 16–17)

For Ms Mulvey, students and parents were not just filling 'empty space' but were actively engaged in constituting, and being constituted by, the spatialities of colonialism and self-determination. Despite appeals, Redfern Primary School was closed, unlike Erskineville Primary School which, with its primarily white student population, remained open despite having lower enrolment numbers than Redfern and other schools that closed. This disparity provokes me to look at more than demographics: to focus on the connections between Aboriginality in the city, inner city schooling, and the policy decisions and structural outcomes related to *Building the Future.*

ABORIGINALITY, 'THE BLOCK', AND URBAN HOPES AND FEARS

The adjacent inner city suburbs of Redfern and Waterloo are significantly disadvantaged according to statistical representations such as indices of deprivation, including unemployment, income, and housing (Australian Bureau of Statistics 2001, South Sydney City Council 2003). Within Redfern is an area known as 'the Block', reputed to be the symbolic centre of urban Aboriginality in Sydney.[4] The Block, which is quite literally one city block, was 'returned' to Aboriginal peoples in 1973 by the newly elected Whitlam Labor government through the establishment of the Aboriginal-controlled Aboriginal Housing Company (AHC). This act of returning land to Aboriginal people was immersed in the politics of land rights, Aboriginal self-determination, and moves away from policies of assimilation (Anderson 1993). The Block is a contested place in the urban imaginary of Sydney, 'presented, simultaneously, as a place of successful Aboriginal political struggle and as an example of failed (urban) Aboriginal self-determination' (Shaw 2000: 291).

On the one hand, the Block was, and is, the material outcome of agitation for Aboriginal rights and recognition, most publicly commenced by the 'Freedom Rides' of 1968 and the associated Black Power movement located in the inner city (Foley 2001). The notion of 'Aboriginal claimed land' adjacent to the Central Business District (CBD) (see Figure 4.1), the administrative heart of the invading colonial power, is a potent symbol of accommodation and resistance and a constant reminder of the illusion of *terra nullius.*[5] On the other hand, the AHC is consistently accused of corruption, to the point that Aboriginality is naturalised as

Figure 4.1 'Rubble from the demolition of a drug house is removed from "the Block", Redfern, Sydney'. The Aboriginal flag is on the wall behind the truck, with Sydney's Central Business District in the background. Photograph: P. Baillie (2004), original photograph held by National Library of Australia.

failure (Shaw 2000). The Block is consistently reported in mainstream media as a 'trouble spot' that needs remedying (see Jull 2004), and the 'Block is presented as Sydney's own "black ghetto" . . ., spiralling out of control and imploding in a sea of drugs and crime' (Shaw 2000: 294). In 2006 only 19 dwellings remain of 102 originally on the land. Many were bulldozed by the AHC in attempts to disperse drug dealing and associated crime.

The depiction of Aboriginality as conflated with danger is a common refrain in this part of the inner city, and Redfern 'remains a feared part of the inner city, even within the . . . context of escalating gentrification' (Shaw 2000: 294). Starting in the 1980s and 1990s, 'social gentrifiers' moved into Redfern and to a lesser extent Waterloo, two suburbs that have historically housed low-income and immigrant families. The 'social gentrifiers' were individuals or couples who purchased and renovated properties (Butler and Robson 2003, following Warde 1991). These gentrifiers replaced the previous occupants of terrace houses who were primarily 1950s and 1960s European migrants, who then moved to larger houses in the outer suburbs of Sydney (Alpin 2000, Darcy 2000).

Figure 4.2 One of the first streets to be socially gentrified in Redfern. '[People] were saying "heh, you know, I don't have enough money to live in Paddington [another inner city suburb], but I can buy one of these Redfern houses cheap, renovate it, . . . I can have my corporate job, my corporate lifestyle, if I'm prepared to put a few bars on the window and be a little careful at night"' (Mr Williams, white, ex-administrator, Redfern Primary). Photograph: K. N. Gulson (2003).

Figure 4.2 shows one of the first streets to be gentrified in Redfern, a street very close to the Central Business District. Redfern and Waterloo were transformed house by house, street by street, creating a diverse range of housing in any one street, such as renovated and dilapidated terraces, new security apartments, and social housing tenements (see Figure 4.3).

While social gentrification continued into the 1990s and 2000s, 'gentrification by capital' (Butler and Robson 2003) or 'third-wave gentrification' (N. Smith 2002) occurred concomitantly. This involved large-scale investment administered through government-corporate arrangements, including a 2003 policy initiative known as the Redfern Renewal Strategy (RRS). This strategy was conceived as 'a holistic approach to addressing urban renewal, economic revitalisation, and improvements in urban amenity' (Redfern Waterloo Partnership Project 2003), with an aim to increase the Redfern Waterloo population by anywhere from 10,000 to 40,000 people over five years. This 'holistic approach' obscures the radical displacement and sanitisation of decay that characterises

Figure 4.3 Housing contrasts in Redfern. Renovated and original terraces are adjacent to new gated security apartments, with a social housing tenement in the background. Photograph: K. N. Gulson (2003).

third-wave gentrification (N. Smith 2002). The Block, due to its location adjacent to Redfern Railway Station, a major transport hub, is repeatedly pinpointed as an impediment to major urban redevelopment like the RRS. Consequently there are constant struggles between the state and the AHC (Gulson and Parkes 2010b, Shaw 2006).[6]

Urban policies like the RRS can be considered the manifestation of 'an array of strategies and projects aimed at consolidating and reinforcing "white" space' (Shaw 2006: 859). In this area of Sydney the educational policy realm as represented by *Building the Future*, can also be included as part of the racialisation of the city and the reinforcement of white space.

SCHOOLING AND THE MARKETISATION OF RACE

Cleveland Street High School and Redfern Primary School were long considered to be schools under threat. Between 1984 and 1991 both schools suffered significant decline in enrolments, with Cleveland Street losing 639 students, and Redfern losing 223 students (see Table 4.1).

Table 4.1   Enrolments (1984–2001) for Cleveland Street High School and Redfern Primary School

School name	Student enrolment by year		
	1984	*1991*	*2001*
Cleveland Street High School	854	215	109
Redfern Primary School	439	216	69

Source: Legislative Council 2002a

Building the Future's key premise was that declining enrolments were brought about through the combination of students moving to non-government schooling and changes in the inner city demographics. There were also references to parents choosing to school their children elsewhere due to lack of curriculum offerings in certain inner city schools. What is noticeable in the *Building the Future* policy documents and in the Legislative Inquiry transcripts is the absence of race and racism from the discussions of structural change. There was no recognition of minor changes in enrolment numbers of Aboriginal students in schools such as Cleveland Street High School and Redfern Primary School. Additionally, there was no acknowledgement that Aboriginal students were considered by some administrators and teachers to be an important, complex, and contradictory factor in the decline of inner city schools. Mr Dunkley, a white, senior administrator at Alexandria Park Community School, previously at Cleveland Street, stated that:

> [Cleveland Street] . . . probably [had] 150 students and most of those students were Aboriginal students, so the Aboriginal population sort of stuck to the school. . . . But the other families . . . gradually chose not to . . . send their kids to that school. That I believe created fairly enormous problems in terms of marginalisation, and residualisation . . . of the Aboriginal students. (Mr Dunkley, Alexandria Park)

Aboriginal students were simultaneously marginalised and exposed. The paramount representation of Cleveland Street was its negative reputation circulating through parental networks and the corporate media. This reputation combined with the dominant Aboriginal student presence to conflate a negative image of the school with negative characterisations of Aboriginal students. This conflation positioned Aboriginal students as detrimental to other students' learning, and an impediment to the 'aspirational' groups in the area. According to Mr Lewis, a white, senior DET bureaucrat who was a key participant in the development of *Building the Future*:

> Cleveland Street was held in pretty poor regard. People saw it as being a largely Aboriginal school . . . and looked for other alternatives. So,

apart from those that had little choice, or weren't all that concerned about what happened . . . the aspirational group within the community looked for alternatives other than Cleveland Street. (Mr Lewis, DET)

Aboriginal students paradoxically appeared to be invisible as 'good students,' while other more 'aspirational' non-Aboriginal students and parents left the school, but not the city. Mr Williams, an ex-senior administrator at Redfern Primary School, suggested many of the people who did not send their children to the inner city schools were the gentrifying, white middle classes. He noted that:

> Redfern Public School had come to have . . . a very bad reputation in the community. It was virtually residualised as an Aboriginal school because . . . enrolment was eighty percent Aboriginal students and none of the white families, and especially the white, moneyed families who'd moved into the area . . . None of those families chose to go, to send their kids to our school because of the reputation it had for violence and bullying and low academic achievement. (Mr Williams, ex-Redfern Primary School administrator)

This connection between Aboriginality, violence, and low achievement parallels the designation of the Block as a place of failure, despair, and decline. As the city gentrified, the connotation of Aboriginality and associated places (the schools, the Block) as failure became more pronounced.

In the Shadow of the Mission

The first *Building the Future* document included a proposal to develop a co-educational years 7–12 school in inner Sydney 'with a special Aboriginal focus . . . [the] proposed name to be Wingara campus' (Legislative Council 2002a: 9). This proposal 'became known almost instantaneously in the local community as "the mission school"' (New South Wales Teachers Federation 2002: 14). A white Teachers Federation representative stated:

> I think one of the alarming aspects of *Building the Future* Mark 1 was Wingara, which was to be a school for predominantly Aboriginal students who were at risk. It was an appropriated Aboriginal name. . . . There was no consultation with the community at all about whether this was an appropriate model. In other words, it was a mission school. That is rightly and properly how the community saw it. (Legislative Council 2002d: 19)

Mission schools had been private church-sponsored institutions on the frontiers of colonial society. These schools were typically where Aboriginal children, many of whom are now known to be part of the 'Stolen

Generations' (Human Rights and Equal Opportunity Commission 1997), had been sent during the era of state-sanctioned assimilation to encourage their conversion, and co-option, into white culture and society (see Choo 2004).

The Wingara proposal was rejected during the *Building the Future* consultation period, at a community meeting in Redfern attended by approximately 400 people, many of them local Aboriginal residents. A commitment was then made to look at another type of K–12 school (Legislative Council 2002b). Mr Lewis recalled that:

> what happened . . . was that the local Aboriginal community saw . . . [Wingara] as setting up a dumping ground for Aboriginal folk and represented it as a mission school, the reestablishment of a mission school, which wasn't the intention and was probably a wrong form of words at the time, but people walked away from that very quickly and said 'righty oh, we'll just trim that off, that's gone, forget about it, Wingara's dead, it's out of the way'. (Mr Lewis, DET)

However, the shadow of the mission casts into relief the idea that Wingara could be 'dead', and 'out of the way'. 'We'll just trim that off, that's gone, forget about it' denies this proposal may have any connotations aside from being somewhat distasteful to Aboriginal people. In the cultural imagination of those white Australians involved in proposing the new school, it is plausible Wingara did not imitate a 'mission school' at all. This new school was to be governed by the state, not the church, and to be built in the heart of urban Sydney.[7] While the experience of oppression and displacement was likely to remain alive in the consciousness of Aboriginal people, this is not necessarily the case for the white majority, who can buy into the 'Great Australian Silence' (Biskup 1982: 12). This silence fosters a belief in a non-eventful 'quiet frontier' free of the 'founding violence' seen in other colonial nations (Veracini 2003: 328). Within this context of an historical amnesia, the DET could remain sensitive to questions of Aboriginal need, and yet claim some ignorance of how the Wingara proposal simply replicated earlier moves in Australia's past, and again implicated education in the practices of assimilation (see also Gulson and Parkes 2009).

Race Viability in the Inner City: Desirable Subjects and the Absent Middle Classes

The next iteration of *Building the Future*, the *Consultation Report* (DET 2001b), proposed the Alexandria Park K-12 Community School. This proposal was developed by the DET with input from open community meetings in the Redfern area. It had some relationship to proposals for a K–12 inner Sydney school raised a number of times in the 1990s by education activists, including Aboriginal people. Alexandria Park, opened in 2003, was created from the closure and amalgamation of Redfern, Waterloo, and Alexandria Primary Schools and Cleveland Street High School. Alexandria Park is now the only remaining public school within three inner city suburbs. The other schools in the area are non-government institutions, some of which are low-fee Catholic systemic schools.

As noted above, despite falling enrolments, a fairly stable Aboriginal student population was maintained in inner city schools. In 2003 Alexandria Park had approximately 240 Aboriginal students out of 337 students, most of these in the K–6 range (Port Jackson District Office 2003). The school provides classes in Aboriginal languages and has become the key centre for the teaching of Aboriginal Studies in the inner Sydney area. Additionally, many Aboriginal parents participate in school decision making. While the Aboriginal student and parent presence was identified as a source of pride at Alexandria Park for both Aboriginal and non-Aboriginal people, this pride was tempered by non-Aboriginal people who suggested the school also needed to reposition itself in order to serve the 'community'.

> We have to remind some of the [school] committee members [who are Aboriginal] that it's not . . . just going to be an Aboriginal school. (Mr Fosdike, white, ex-Redfern Primary School teacher, now Alexandria Park)

> A tension [will be] to see how . . . focused the new school will be in terms of Aboriginal education. . . . Because if you want to broaden the base and get all of the local kids attending then you've got to be inclusive but if you lose your focus on Aboriginal education you're going to alienate the Aboriginal community. So there's a real tension there between trying to get a school that has more kids in it, you know a broader spectrum . . . that's not residualised and also that still focuses on . . . community. (Mr Williams, ex- Redfern Primary School teacher)

> [The aim of Alexandria Park is] to try and have a brand new, bright, shiny, attractive option to people locally, and by doing that have it not seen as a ghetto like arrangement that was just there servicing one section of the community, but a school serving all the community. (Mr Lewis, DET)

The notion of 'community' dichotomises Aboriginal and non-Aboriginal students. It is a fraught construction in the context of the racialisation of the inner city and the previously closed inner city schools. The requirement of revitalisation of the Alexandria Park school 'product' under *Building the Future* operates to distinguish it from the 'ghetto-Aboriginal-dangerous' constitution of the previous schools and areas like the Block. The new Alexandria Park school must dilute the previously residualised, Aboriginal dominated, inner city schools that were closed. If it does this Alexandria Park can be a successful school with an Aboriginal presence but unsuccessful if Aboriginal dominated.

The former allows the school to be a 'bright, shiny' option, a distinction that is reinforced by connecting the school's future to the ongoing gentrification of the inner city. Mr Lewis stated the school had:

> developed a structure and capacity to reinvent ourselves and I think that's profoundly important . . . if we are really going to match the changing expectations of the local community, and deliver to our new client group. We have to consciously plan, to reinvent ourselves, continuously. (Mr Lewis, DET)

However, what is clear from the rationale for *Building the Future* is the DET considered the inner city as increasingly populated with young professionals. These were not to be the present and future target group for public schools in the inner city. Urban change, at least according to *Building the Future*, brought in the childless. Nonetheless, in contradiction to the DET, people involved with the Alexandria Park school were convinced urban change would also provide potential 'new clients'.

I wish to be clear that I am not concerned with whether there was a change in the actual numbers of white, middle-class students in the inner city or in Alexandria Park school. Rather what interests me is how white, middle-class inner city and educational subjects can be constituted as desirable new clients in this inner city education market. While *Building the Future* aimed to 'revitalise' inner city schooling, one of the aims of the Alexandria Park school in gentrifying inner Sydney became repositioning itself as a particular product. Gentrification and the idea of a positive social mix (Byrne 2003) was drawn upon by those associated with the Alexandria Park School to reposition the types of students that they saw as central to its remit. Gentrification in this education market equated with 'middle class' and desirable students. The 'pre-gentrified' equated with Aboriginal students and undesirable burdens.

Reconfiguring Aboriginal Students as the Entrepreneurial Norm

As noted above, when the new Alexandria Park school opened it already had many Aboriginal inner city students. These students needed to be accommodated, or co-opted, into the DET's project of inner city education revitalisation. In giving evidence to the Legislative Inquiry the white, then Director General of the DET, Dr Ken Boston, claimed:

> [t]he vision for the school was . . . that [it] offered excellence in Aboriginal education but [the school] would be so good that it would attract back to the public education system the middle-class non-Aboriginal families of the area. (Legislative Council 2002b: 11)

This is quite a disturbing construction, where a school that offers Aboriginal education simultaneously needs to be 'so good' it can overcome the taint of Aboriginality. This idea of the school offering 'excellence' for both Aboriginal and non-Aboriginal students underpins the introduction of academic streaming within the school. The school instigated 'a program to identify Aboriginal students who are underachieving despite possessing high academic potential' (Fenton and Myers 2006: 3). Part of this provision is an Opportunity Class (OC) for Years 5 and 6. OCs aim to provide 'gifted and talented' students a more stimulating intellectual environment than 'mainstream' classes. The Alexandria Park OC is also proposed as one way of revitalising the school and, more broadly, inner city public education, by projecting an image of academic rigour and excellence for both Aboriginal and non-Aboriginal students.[8] Mr Lewis noted the school has tried:

> to increasingly meet the expectations of all of the local community, and to do that we've built into it an OC provision for years 5 and 6 ... and what's a bit different with this OC provision is that [the school has] said 'righty oh, we'll offer twenty five of the thirty places each year in the usual way, but we'll keep five places or roughly 20 percent of the enrolment that we'll use for gifted and talented [Aboriginal] students that we identify in other ways, largely by nomination from their schools or by nomination from parents, and then we'll have a look at them and see whether they'd benefit from the program and if it's believed that they would, they'll be slotted straight in'. So what we're trying to do is to really demonstrate to the broader community, and to the Aboriginal community in particular, that we recognise that we've got gifted and talented Aboriginal students, and we're doing something about it, and making that quite visible, and I think that's an important initiative. (Mr Lewis, DET)

This class is selected on the basis of a standardised test that can be sat by interested non-Aboriginal students within and outside the school. In addition to the school-based recommendations noted by Mr Lewis, Aboriginal students are assessed for suitability using the ' Coolabah Dynamic Assessment Method . . . which creates a non-threatening and culturally unbiased environment where students solve a variety of puzzles in groups of four' (Fenton and Myers 2006: 3).

Equality of opportunity, framed within academic excellence, applies to those Aboriginal students who are deemed to be 'bright', but are still different from non-Aboriginal students, a differentiation based on the mode of entry to the OC. As Mr Lewis noted, recommendations of potential Aboriginal students are sought from schools, which on the one hand allows Aboriginal students to be identified who may have previously been disadvantaged by other forms of testing. On the other hand there is evidence from the UK that teachers make judgements about academic ability on the basis of race, with invidious consequences for some students of colour who are deemed to lack the requisite academic potential (e.g., Gillborn and Youdell 2000).

Furthermore, the OC reconfigures differentiation between Aboriginal students, not just between Aboriginal and non-Aboriginal students. While this acknowledges the heterogeneity of Aboriginal students, it also appears to distinguish between desirable and undesirable Aboriginal students. Mr Nicks stated that:

> we've got a lot of other [Aboriginal] kids come to us, but they're kids who are coming because they're on about the type of teaching that we're doing, or the high expectations of [Aboriginal] kids or the work in Aboriginal languages, or the work in Aboriginal studies and so there might be a more aspirational [Aboriginal] person who is, is starting to come to us. (Mr Nicks, Alexandria Park)

Alexandria Park Community School will be a place for Aboriginal students who are considered *all* the 'same, that is Aboriginal, but also differentiated: 'bright' and 'aspirational' entrepreneurial individuals, as opposed, one assumes, to the 'non-bright' and 'non-aspirational' Aboriginal students who are already in the school or who may attend in the future.

Aboriginal students were 'unmarketable' when attending schools such as Redfern Primary School. Conversely, the *Building the Future* restructuring created the new Alexandria Park Community School and now provides the conditions of opportunity for the constitution of a new type of inner city educational subject. In the differentiated school, programmes such as the OC reconstitutes Aboriginal students as 'marketable,' conditional on fulfilling the requirements of the neoliberal educational subject. These are Aboriginal student subjectivities that, arguably, fit the desired white, middle-class practices of schooling in education markets (Ball 2003, Gewirtz 2001, Reay 2008, Youdell 2006). These students then become markers, and marketable examples, of what can be done with 'recalcitrant' Aboriginal populations through education policy.

PROBLEMATISING ABORIGINALITY, THE CITY, AND SCHOOLING

> [D]uring the Olympics we had a lot of reporters from all over the world [visit the Block]. . . . Fifteen interviews a day I used to do . . . just during those two weeks . . . and we had this French guy, I had to throw him out of the office, he was such a moron. . . . [H]e said, 'You know, I've been in Redfern for a week, and I haven't seen one Aboriginal'. I said 'Man, you walked past four of them as you walked in the fucking office'. He said, 'They weren't Aboriginal'. I said, 'What are you talking about? French people aren't all the same, we have white Aboriginal, we have dark Aboriginal, we have in between, we have short, tall, everything'. He said, 'Nah, I want to see the Aboriginal with the thing there, the spear' and I said 'You know

what? You're too fucking stupid!' (Non-Aboriginal member of the
Aboriginal Housing Company)

In this chapter I explored how *Building the Future* was inexorably linked
to the changing inner city of Sydney. I identified two key connections:
one, the mobilisation of demographics to justify the restructuring of public schooling; and, two, the identification, in racialised policy practices,
of gentrification as a positive aspect of urban change which would provide new white, middle-class students. I noted that the very inner city and
educational subjects that are desired by the Alexandria Park school, 'middle-class' and 'non-Aboriginal', are present through gentrification and
physically absent from the school. People associated with the Alexandria
Park school proudly acknowledge the 'non–middle class' and Aboriginal presence in the school; however, the convergence of gentrification
with educational policy directions such as markets constitute new desires
about who are 'ideal' urban and educational subjects. It is this tension
that underscores my concluding comments in this chapter.

As the epigraph commencing this chapter suggests, Aboriginal people
living in urban environments like Redfern are typically forced to deal with
multiple and contradictory attributions of contemporary Aboriginality. In
the case of schooling in the inner city of Sydney, Aboriginality is located
within market discourses that shape one (but not every) set of possibilities
about who Aboriginal students are encouraged to be in inner city schooling. The Alexandria Park Community School has a focus on Aboriginal
students, such as offering Aboriginal languages curriculum. It also aims
to provide Aboriginal students with an education equal to that of non-
Aboriginal students, with the OC a salient example. This construction of
the entrepreneurial Aboriginal student is thus partially posited within the
bounds of white-defined success, connected to the logics of colonialism.
Therefore, the dual aim of the school runs the risk of replicating a particular problem predicted by postcolonial theory. The power of colonial
discourse was not just its strategy of constructing the colonised subject as
'different and other within the categories of knowledge of the West' (Hall
1997: 112), but manifested more profoundly in its ability to make the colonised see themselves as 'the Other' (see also Young 1990).

Thus, what I finish this chapter with is the idea of the 'highly contested
terrain' of Aboriginality, between essentialised and constructed identities
(Pettman 1995: 75), a contested terrain evident in the cultural politics of
urban places and urban schooling. Morgan suggests:

> [t]raditionalism and essentialism are double-edged swords. On the one
> hand, they allow Indigenous city dwellers to define a distinctive space
> for their culture and politics to claim legitimacy based on ancient at-
> tachments. On the other hand, they have the effect of obscuring the re-
> worked, contemporary residual forms of Indigenous culture and social

life. They make urban Aboriginal people vulnerable to attacks from those who question their authenticity. (Morgan 2006: 153)

Nonetheless, on this contested terrain the strategic mobilisation of Aboriginality is a crucial way of building political momentum in battles over the future of inner city Aboriginal peoples. This includes the assertion that the Block is an important designate of Aboriginal self-determination in contemporary political life, and securing an Aboriginal place in schooling, as noted by Ms Mulvey in her evidence to the Legislative Inquiry (above). The Block and Alexandria Park Community School serve as powerful, provisional and fraught motifs of accomplished and potential self-determination.

5 Policy, Aspirations, and Urban Imaginaries in East London

Excellence in Cities . . . tackles the particular problems facing children in our cities . . . it aims to raise the aspirations and achievements of pupils and to tackle disaffection, social exclusion, truancy and indiscipline and improve parents' confidence in cities. (Department for Education and Skills 2003b)

After being elected in 1997, the Blair Labour government introduced a number of area-based initiatives across social and urban policy realms. These initiatives were policy interventions aimed at redressing social and spatial exclusion in deprived areas (Cochrane 2007, Lupton 2009). *Excellence in Cities* was one such initiative in education, introduced in 1999 and discontinued in 2006, which the Department for Education and Skills (DfES)[1] proposed to address long-term educational disadvantage and underachievement in schools in deprived urban areas (DfES 2003b, Stoney et al. 2002). *Excellence in Cities* was intended to complement other urban programmes, including the Single Regeneration Budget, New Deal for Communities, and the Neighbourhood Regeneration Strategy (Office for Standards in Education 2003a).

In March 1999, the DfES incorporated the Local Education Authority (LEA) of Tower Hamlets into an *Excellence in Cities* partnership. There were only two criteria for a LEA to be integrated into an *Excellence in Cities* partnership: 24 percent or more students were receiving Free School Meals (FSMs), a fairly crude indicator of student poverty; and the LEA was in an urban area (DfES, 2003b). 62 percent of Tower Hamlets LEA students were eligible for FSMs (Tower Hamlets LEA 2003), and the LEA was in East London.

One aspect of the *Excellence in Cities* programme was the creation of *Excellence in Cities* Action Zones. These zones were derived from, and in some cases supplanted, Education Action Zones (EAZs) which combined secondary and primary schools under one relatively flexible administrative structure, with an emphasis on increasing private sector involvement in education (Dickson and Power 2001, Gamarnikow and Green 1999). Three *Excellence in Cities* zones were created in Tower Hamlets. In 2003, the Poplar *Excellence in Cities* zone replaced the Poplar EAZ. The new zone incorporated five primary schools and one secondary school: Bygrove,

Culloden, Lansbury Lawrence, Manorfield, and Mayflower Primary Schools and Langdon Park Secondary School.[2]

In this chapter, I connect policy, aspirations, and geographical imaginations to consider the relationships between schooling and place. To do this, I first tease out the contrasts between two adjacent areas of Tower Hamlets: Poplar, an isolated and relatively impoverished area, and Canary Wharf, a hub for multinational financial companies. I then explore the connections between Canary Wharf and Poplar, with a focus on corporate participation in the Poplar *Excellence in Cities* Action Zone. The latter part of the chapter explores how white, middle-class aspirations are drawn upon in attempts to inspire Poplar students to achieve academically and raise general educational standards in Tower Hamlets. I suggest a form of geographical imagining ties these aspirations to Canary Wharf, an imagining which encourages the take-up of desirable neoliberal educational subjectivities.

POVERTY, RACE, AND DECLINE

Poplar has been designated one of the most impoverished areas in Tower Hamlets, which itself is one of the poorest boroughs in England (Hall 2007). Poplar is an area with a number of small council housing estates, limited amounts of private housing that are often part of the 'right-to-buy' scheme that transferred council housing to private ownership, small-scale industries, and a somewhat run-down marketplace. Urban regeneration programs in the 2000s renovated and replaced some existing housing stock, along with providing amenities such as playgrounds and community centres, and increased community social services (Hall 2007 Leaside Regeneration Ltd 2003). Despite this regeneration, the circumstances for many Poplar residents are highly stressful, particularly on the housing estates which:

> are characterized by high levels of poverty and benefit dependency. Two thirds of households include an individual in receipt of some form of benefit whereas one tenth have no use of *any* of the following: phone, washing machine, drying facilities, study space, cable or satellite TV, a lift, a private garden or a balcony. (Hall 2007: 261, original emphasis)

Poplar is surrounded and sliced by major through-roads, concrete promises of moving elsewhere in the United Kingdom and Europe. Railways and canals, emblematic of nineteenth-century industrialisation, carve up the landscape. These physical features reinforce a sense of insularity, obsoleteness, and isolation in Poplar, a point noted by many school administrators and teachers.

> [T]he quality of the housing stock and the quality of amenities, in the whole of [Poplar] . . . had been allowed to deteriorate and of course

that has a direct impact on . . . the people who live here and the people who want to live here. So anybody who could get out had got out really and [Poplar] was gradually being left with either people who had nowhere else to go, or people who were being shipped through. (Ms Gerrard, white administrator, Culloden Primary School)

[Poplar. . .] as well as being enormously diverse, it's insular at the same time. And the children we have here you'll find don't leave Poplar at all, I mean physically. And they've got an idea of other places in London or this, that and the other but . . . they don't really get out much. (Mr Bellamy, white teacher, Langdon Park Secondary School)

This combination of insularity and being left behind is, in part, a white perspective. According to the 2001 Census the white[3] population in Tower Hamlets was 52.4 percent compared with 90.9 percent in England (Office of National Statistics 2001). In Poplar this was 41.5 percent.

The borough's school population had increased by 16.9 percent over the period 1991 to 2001, with Bangladeshi students the largest group (14.4 percent). Various immigration policies and public housing strategies, over a period of 40 years, resulted in a large proportion of England's Bangladeshi population residing in Tower Hamlets (see Foster 1999). There is also some evidence that part of the Caribbean and the white populations were leaving Poplar, with a 13.3 percent decrease in Caribbean and white English, Scottish, and Welsh students between 1991 and 2001 (Poplar Zone 2000: 4).

In 2003, 69 percent of students were non-white at Bygrove Primary School (Office for Standards in Education 2003b). Mr Wright, a white, senior administrator at Bygrove, stated:

we've changed from being a predominantly white school to an increasingly bilingual, ethnic minority school and I think that reflects the area. . . . And part of the change from a predominantly white population has been the more prosperous and the better educated and the more ambitious parents are the ones who've moved out. They've moved out to more suburban areas and we have more ethnic minority families moving in. (Mr Wright, Bygrove Primary School)

The 'ambitious' people moving out are primarily white, indicative of an 'East Ender white flight' from the inner city to the outer parts of London and surrounding counties such as Essex (Eade 1997). Moreover, there was tension between the 'ethnic minority' families and a remnant white population in Poplar who 'have not got out'. Mr Beckham, a white teacher at Bygrove, outlined how:

the people who don't seem to be happy are the white working class families because they feel that their area, the words they use is 'invaded' by the proportion of [Bangladeshi] families who seem to be moving into the area . . . and I've dealt with specific cases of racism where parents have said 'I do not want my child to sit next to that brown child'. . . . And I've come across bad integration cases where there's big blocks of just [Bangladeshi] parents and then one or two white working class families moving in and then there's been . . . racism going on in between them. Because we find [one part of Poplar] it's nicknamed Little Calcutta, which is in India, but Little Calcutta for the [Bangladeshi] area. And this side, the [marketplace] is predominantly white. There appears to be a sort of clear divide and they don't seem to like wanting to mix too much either. (Mr Beckham, Bygrove Primary School)

The anti-Bangladeshi attitudes need to be contextualised both within the extensive Bangladeshi immigration into the UK and Tower Hamlets (Eade 1997) and, more generally, within resentment, racism and violence against non-whites. The latter is implicated in the discourse of the white working class as victims of disproportionate, state-imposed, race equality measures (Gillborn and Kirton 2000, Gillborn 2010b). Hesse (1997) examines how racial violence in British cities can be connected to Cohen's (1988) idea of 'neighbourhood nationalism', which reifies the idea of white legitimacy and rights to the city. This nationalism:

ascribes 'illegitimacy' to the presence of Asian and Black people in the 'locality'. It is invoked randomly and opportunistically in a range of forms in order to disrupt the incorporation of a racially proscribed 'other' within a proprietorial sense of place. (Hesse 1997: 89)

Defence of nostalgia and the imaginary nation underpins schooling and neighbourhood. Poplar represents an ever-shrinking island of whiteness in a sea of change: the tide of substantial immigration into Tower Hamlets and of hyper-wealth represented by the adjacent Canary Wharf.

CANARY WHARF AS URBAN SUPERIMPOSITION

It feels strange to be returning to Canary Wharf six years after my doctoral fieldwork. I catch the Jubilee tubeline from Waterloo and when I alight at Canary Wharf I exit out of the cavernous tube station, up the escalators and emerge into the Canary Wharf square. I am greeted with a view of water, an electronic information ticker and a giant television informing me about the latest news, most of which is related to the movements of the global financial market. Here, people hurry, primarily in business attire, from the station to the surrounding office buildings. These buildings are emblazoned with the names of global financial services and banks—Barclays, HSBC, Citi. . . . And I cannot help but notice that most of the faces of people in suits are white. (K.N. Gulson, field notes, October 2009)

Figure 5.1   The square outside Canary Wharf tube station. Photograph: K. N. Gulson (2009).

Canary Wharf is the financial hub of the 'Docklands' on the banks of the Thames River. The 'Docklands' had its origins in the 1970s when the working docks were closed, and targeted for redevelopment including new industries and investment in public housing (Eade 2000). However, in the 1980s these social aims were superseded when the Thatcher Conservative government created the London Docklands Development Corporation (LDDC). The LDDC combined an enormous influx of government funds and global capital, with £2041 million of public funds, and £6227 million of private sector funds. A total of £8268 million was outlayed between 1981 and 1996 to build a corporate monolith (Foster 1999). After nearly thirty years of development the buildings of Canary Wharf dominate the London skyline, housing mulitnational financial groups such as Citigroup[4], entertainment facilities, mid- to high-end retail outlets and residential buildings (see Figure 5.2).

Through the late 1980s and into the early 1990s, there was significant conflict between the LDCC which posited the 'Docklands' as a global development, and the desires of local residents and other activists to retain the 'old' East End, especially on the Isle of Dogs where Canary Wharf is now located (see Bird 1993, Massey 1994a). Massey (1994a) argues the opposition to the LDDC was bifurcated. The first aspect of resistance to urban development involved recourse to a 'local' essence strongly resonant of a working-class East End. Identifying the East End in this way meant rejecting 'yuppie' newcomers associated with the 'Docklands'. The second aspect

Figure 5.2   Canary Wharf from Poplar. '[I]n a deliberate echo of the World Trade Center, New York's post-docks office complex, the grandiloquent phallic towers of the Canary Wharf "office city" emerged to change . . . the London skyline' (Blake 2008: 228). Photograph: K. N. Gulson (2009).

depended on identifying the East End as *white* and working class, even if this did not represent the actuality of large scale immigration over many years. As noted, housing policies were settling large numbers of Bangladeshi migrants in Tower Hamlets, including the Isle of Dogs and Poplar. The white population rejected *these* 'newcomers' on the grounds that they were counter to an 'authentic white' East End (see also Massey 2005). Opposition to Canary Wharf thus both separated and converged around opposition to 'newcomers' who were already in *and* outside place.

Cohen (1997) argues that Canary Wharf was put forward by supporters as a way to ameliorate such conflict, rather than development as the actual focus of racialised invocations. Cohen considers that with Canary Wharf:

> we are offered a vision of harmonious reintegration of east and west, an area where rich yuppies and poor cockneys, Bangladeshi and white English families could happily co-exist within pleasurable reach of each other's otherness and without treading on each other's toes. This was one of the key plots through which the inside story of the area's development was told from the vantage point of outsiders. At the same time this official iconography of multiculturalism was projected onto a narrative map of modernity, progress, and urban regeneration in which the presence of the poor, the unemployed, the elderly, indeed almost anyone who did not conform to the dominant image of the economically active entrepreneur, was effectively sidelined. (Cohen 1997: 77–78)

It is this early story of progress, urban change, and the eliding of conflict associated with Canary Wharf that can also be extended into the twenty-first century through reference to education policy and schooling in Poplar. Before moving to this explication, in the next section I want to reinforce the stark contrasts characteristic of this area of London. I do this in a multi-textual manner, which includes an ethnographic pastiche of field notes, photographs, and interview transcripts.[5]

'A GODFORSAKEN AREA': ON THE CONTIGUITY OF POPLAR AND CANARY WHARF

> I catch the Docklands Light Rail from Canary Wharf and embark at the Poplar station. I turn south, remembering it is almost impossible to walk directly to Canary Wharf, even though it is less than half a kilometre away. A freeway and construction sites stand in the way—there is a pedestrian overpass but I see no one walking over this and it appears to end in a vacant lot. The office buildings on Canary Wharf dwarf me and the surrounding buildings in Poplar. When I alight the light rail platform a wave of people hits me—it is

lunch break at the Tower Hamlets College and there are far fewer white faces here, and much broader accents, than I heard on Canary Wharf. There are large groups of young men of colour, and I realise that I feel out of place. I am here to take photos and I feel like, well I am, a voyeur. Yet I continue because this is what I am here for—to be reminded again, six years later, of the contrasts between Canary Wharf and Poplar that first struck me in 2003. (K. N. Gulson, field notes, October 2009)

[Poplar] is a godforsaken area, nobody comes to it. . . . We're very isolated here and I've watched Canary Wharf grow, but you won't hear the people here talking about going to Docklands. This is a very isolated community, an apathetic community and the people don't go out of it, so in some ways the development of the Docklands hasn't affected us here at all. (Ms Rooney, white administrator, Manorfield Primary School)

[Students] (shrugs shoulders) like that [when Canary Wharf is mentioned], it's no big deal. . . its just it's not anything that's going to offer them much, that's the impression I get . . . the old East End is more important to them than this new East End. (Ms Fowler, white, former teacher, Langdon Park Primary School)

Figure 5.3 Canary Wharf from Tower Hamlets College at the southern edge of Poplar. The light rail station is in the mid-ground. Photograph: K. N. Gulson (2003).

Figure 5.4   A bypass separating Poplar from Canary Wharf. In this part of East London, physical barriers become social metonyms; the landscape reinforces a sense of disparity between Poplar and Canary Wharf. A road is to be negotiated as something to cross and reinforces a lack of social and economic parity or mobility. Photograph: K. N. Gulson (2003).

> I don't think it's a place for . . . my kind. I see Canary Wharf as like a business peoples' place, I don't really see it as a place for youngsters. When I go there I feel out of place really, that's why I don't really go there a lot. . . . Most of the people there . . . think that they're better than you kind of thing or that's how they carry themselves. That's how they make themselves look, like they're all snobby and that, most people there. Or that's how I see it anyway, that's my personal view . . . they kind of turn their nose up at you. (Reggie, white, 16-year old male youth, Langdon Secondary School)

> [T]here was a very . . . big feeling of being very close to a . . . centre of wealth, and yet having no access to it at all, and almost it having a really detrimental effect on the area. (Ms Gerrard, Culloden Primary School)

While Canary Wharf is simultaneously adjacent to and remote from Poplar, there are other ways in which Canary Wharf is a significant presence in Poplar. This includes the openings provided by *Excellence in Cities* that encouraged increased business participation in schooling.

Figure 5.5   Capital is the background to Poplar's poverty. The headquarters of Barclays Bank on Canary Wharf, with council housing in Poplar in the foreground. Photograph: K. N. Gulson (2009).

EDUCATION POLICY, CORPORATIONS, AND PROPITIOUS PLACES

Canary Wharf reinforces the relative deprivation of the Poplar area, yet it also represents a connection to global flows, to mobility, and to possibilities and unlimited horizons; it is a connection to a chance for something different. With significant influxes of global capital and with many transnational corporations housed there, Canary Wharf might be seen as the enactment and perhaps paradoxically the emplacement of globalisation. Here, I work broadly from the idea of globalisation as 'a making of space(s), an active reconfiguration and meeting-up through practices and relations of a multitude of trajectories' (Massey 2005: 83).

In this section I propose that educational policy positioned Canary Wharf as a central component of educational endeavours in Poplar. Specifically I examine how *Excellence in Cities* operated as a policy permission that invited the global corporate sector on Canary Wharf into Poplar schools. To explore this permission, this invitation, I focus on the philanthropic aspects of corporate involvement, notably the role of Citigroup, a global financial services corporation.

Corporations, Education, and Banality

> Given the popular perception of the corporate sector as greed-driven and uninterested in the wider public good, corporate public relations are increasingly designed to counteract poor reputations. Schools are a particularly good place for corporations to do this sort of ideological work and to establish a philanthropic image. (Kenway and Bullen 2001: 100)

The Poplar *Excellence in Cities* Action Zone, as part of the Tower Hamlets *Excellence in Cities* partnership, had a central mission to enable 'local partnerships to . . . develop innovative and radical solutions [to] . . . raise educational standards' (DfES, 2003a). These 'local partnerships' preferably involved the private sector. Each *Excellence in Cities* Action Zone would receive £50,000 from the DfES if they raised money or obtained 'in-kind' time from the private sector (DfES, 2003a). In Poplar, the links between individual corporations on Canary Wharf and the schools in the *Excellence in Cities* Action Zone were and continue to be made through organisations such as the Education Business Partnerships (EBP). This is a charity operating out of the Tower Hamlets LEA that encourages the private sector to work with schools (http://www.thebp.org/).

The EBP set up the initial arrangements between schools in the Poplar zone and Citigroup, which runs community outreach programmes. One outcome was that Citigroup employees participated in a reading programme in some Poplar schools. On Tuesdays and Wednesdays approximately a dozen Citigroup employees attended Bygrove Primary for half an hour to listen to Year 1 and 2 students read. Mr White, an administrator at Bygrove, considered this initial interaction between the school and Citigroup as vital in eliciting a £14,000 contribution by the Citigroup Foundation[6] for a computer room built at the school. This contribution was matched by £14,000 from the DfES. Many people in the Poplar zone highlighted this partnership as a model arrangement of public-private co-operation. However, this contribution can also be seen relative to Citigroup's financial scope. Citigroup contributed £14,000, whilst the total net income for 2002 for the Citigroup financial group, world-wide, was US$15.28 billion (Citigroup 2003). The minor presence of Citigroup in the Poplar zone mirrors the relative triviality and banality of corporate participation in EAZs (Power et al. 2004). Nevertheless, while the role of corporations such as Citigroup in schools appears relatively small in financial terms, the banal, the mundane, the everyday, the face-to-face contacts, can be as notable as monetary exchange in the dynamics of public-private partnerships.

'It's not about money. It's about hope'

A focus on the cultural practices of seemingly mundane interactions between Citigroup and schools generates the possibility of rethinking the corporate-school relationship in Poplar, and corporate involvement in schooling more generally.

Citigroup's connections to schools are part of a tradition of US philanthropy where 'outreach into the community was part of everyday business' (Ms Kewell, white employee, Citigroup community development). There is a convergence between this outreach work and a policy environment, such as *Excellence in Cities*, that permits corporate involvement in public institutions. The introduction of corporations into the educational sector is part of what Ball (2007) identifies as the development of new policy communities under successive Labour governments. These communities are underpinned by a complex intersection of:

> the import of American-style corporate philanthropy and the use of 'positional investments' by business organisations and the 'acting out' of corporate social responsibility. . . . There is a complex overlapping of philanthropy, influence and business interests. (Ball 2007: 122–123)

These policy communities obscure where business ends and philanthropy begins, and complicate the functions, intents, and outcomes of corporate work labelled as philanthropy. Is it business or philanthropy when corporations establish fruitful relationships with the state that may result in ongoing contractual relationships, and tax incentives, outside of the initial terms of contact? (Ball 2007). In relation to the Poplar zone, Ms Kewell recalled that the Citigroup chairman for Europe attended the opening of the computer suite at Bygrove Primary School, which, as noted above, was partially funded by Citigroup.

> My chairman actually. . . [went] to Bygrove Primary and we did . . . a launch opening of the computer lab with [a government minister], which was kind of nice . . . for our employees to spend time with [our chairman . . .]. Our chairman for Europe is obviously . . . quite a busy guy and for them to . . . spend time with him, and then for him to see . . . that people . . . stood behind this kind of [voluntary] commitment, employees were kind of directly connected with what we're doing on this totally different level, he found that to be really helpful. And of course . . . it was nice for him to see the minister. (Ms Kewell, Citigroup)

The CEO is thus able to observe the results of donations by the Citigroup philanthropic arm, the work of the employee volunteers, and, almost as an afterthought, as happenstance, take the opportunity to network with a government minister.

Individual workers who volunteer as readers in schools like Bygrove are donating their time. Nonetheless, when the chairman is in attendance, this volunteering is effective corporate behaviour, an earning of 'credit' for community outreach work. Ball (2007) notes that volunteering, these in-kind donations of employee generosity, is important to some companies for 'retaining and motivating staff as well as playing its part in making up "portfolios of philanthropic investments" which may contribute to the promotion or legitimation of corporate brands' (p.126). When the emphasis is the latter, even community outreach programmes are another global market within which to compete.

> And frankly I think if you talk to a bunch of different . . . [mulitnational] companies, I think . . . [we] have a lot to learn from some of these companies, because I think in some senses their penetration rate is better than . . . [our] penetration rate. (Ms Kewell, Citigroup)

In addition to increasing employee involvement, from this position the 'community' is something to penetrate through the practices of *competitive* philanthropy. The tensions between different functions of Citigroup become evident in the practices of philanthropy. The Citigroup Foundation states, in terms of its participation in education, that: 'It's not about money. It's about hope' (Citigroup Foundation 2003). Nonetheless, while this multinational corporation generates 'hope' through its regional community outreach and organisationally distinct philanthropic foundation, philanthropy also contributes to the core business of a global merchant bank which *is* all about money.

EDUCATION POLICY AND THE POLITICS OF ASPIRATION

A number of teachers and administrators in Poplar connected educational achievement and aspirations with social mobility and the alleviation of poverty. Mr Bellamy, of Langdon Park Secondary School, in talking about the Poplar zone, stated its primary purpose was:

> to raise levels of achievement . . . within the school, so that the children leaving here will gain better qualifications and be able to share in the prosperity, 'cause there are . . . jobs available around here. But people from around here haven't gone on to further education, so haven't been able to get the well-paid jobs, [they've] been getting the service jobs. So I think [with the zone] long term you'll have a better-qualified community and a more prosperous community. (Mr Bellamy, Langdon Park Secondary School)

This fits neatly within New Labour's discursive approach to education and social exclusion. Schooling, standards and social inequality form part of the 'success against the odds' assumption that raising academic standards will address social inequalities (Jones 2003: 171). The *Excellence in Cities* policy, for example, states 'it aims to raise the aspirations and achievements of pupils' (DfES 2003b). Ms Talon, a white member of the Tower Hamlets *Excellence in Cities* programme, stated that the focus of the Poplar zone should be on the students rather than improving quality of life in Poplar, for:

> the thing . . . the zone must focus on [is] . . . its pupils . . . and the key is to look at what . . . is preventing those pupils from really taking hold of their learning opportunities and running with them and opening up their horizons and aiming for everything and anything. That's. . .the key question that the zone must always ask itself. . . . It is not [the zone's] remit to actually . . . have as their main focus improving the . . . quality of life in that area. It isn't, it should impact on that by driving at the children. (Ms Talon, Tower Hamlets *Excellence in Cities*)

I am not disputing the possibility, or desirability, of Poplar students achieving high academic results. Furthermore, I do not want to diminish young people's aspirations, dreams, and the significance of hope. However, I am suggesting that when aspirations are posited as central to raising educational achievement and standards, then this premise warrants interrogation.

Aspirations As a Policy Aim and Technology

> How much talent that could flourish is lost through a poverty of aspiration? Wasted not because young talents fail to reach the stars but because they grow up with no stars to reach? (Prime Minister Gordon Brown, Speech to Labour Party Conference, 2007, cited in Raco 2009)

The residents and students of Poplar are designated as populations at risk. Dean (1999) identifies how advanced liberal governments mobilise particular rationalities and technologies of risk, through which a division, albeit it fluid, can be discerned 'between active citizens (capable of managing their own risk) and targeted populations (disadvantaged groups, the "at risk", the high risk) who require intervention in the management of risks' (Dean 1999: 167). The students, and indirectly the parents, in Poplar schools comprise one of these target populations. Educational policy such as *Excellence in Cities*, while identifying educational standards as a primary goal, also aims to reconstitute these populations as active citizens, in order to manage their own risks. This includes managing learning, achievement, and more broadly decisions of health and employment. Dean (1999) argues this reconstitution is part of the technologies of agency, or more specifically, technologies of citizenship (following Cruickshank 1993, 1994). These technologies encompass techniques that focus on self-esteem and discourses of empowerment, encouraging processes of consultation and practices of negotiation.

> These technologies of citizenship engage us as active and free citizens, as informed and responsible consumers, as members of self-managing communities and organizations, as actors in democratizing social movements, and as agents capable of taking control of our own risks. (Dean 1999: 168)

Thus, social policies, like *Excellence in Cities*, encourage students and parents to manage their own risks by coupling aspirations with academic achievements. As part of the policy practices associated with *Excellence in Cities*, aspirations contribute to rationalities and technologies connected to the reforms of the welfare state. What constitutes these types of reforms:

> are a series of discourses and narratives about citizenship and the ways in which state action can both create and inhibit the development of 'aspirational' citizens, eager to take on greater responsibility for themselves and the well-being of their communities. (Raco 2009: 436)

Raco (2009) identifies how successive Labour governments in the UK shifted from a politics of expectation to a politics of aspiration. Traditional forms of citizenship, characterised as 'expectational citizenship', ostensibly resulted in a 'poverty of aspirations'. Conversely reconfiguring citizenship seems to align entrepreneurial subjects with the take-up of 'aspirational citizenship' (p. 438).

The object of aspiration, the desired outcome, is to become the middle-class consumer (Raco 2009). This parallels what Gewirtz (2001) highlights as an aim of Labour education policies, for working-class parents to become consumers of schooling. These parents (and students) are thus to replicate the ideal of middle-class parental practices, and the ideal of the middle-class student, to consequently become aspiring, entrepreneurial subjects. Additionally, schools play a key role as 'central agents in providing students with repertoires through which they can make sense of themselves, what they do, and why they do it' (O'Flynn and Petersen 2007: 461). Teachers are simultaneously positioned as experts and de-professionalised as part of the performative functions of accountability, inherent in the move towards standards, and the monitoring and reporting of educational achievement (Ball 2000, Webb 2005, 2006).

While much of the work about the middle classes and education markets has focused on middle-class parents (e.g., Reay 2008), of note here are white, middle-class teachers as arbiters *of* and *as* ideal neoliberal subjects. In 2000–2001 86.2 percent of teachers were identified as white in inner London LEAs (Ross 2002: 104). Students in Poplar are likely to encounter an overwhelming majority of white teachers and administrators. To my mind, the supplanting of expectations with the politics of aspirations conceivably accords with a white, middle-class orientation.

The marketised realm of policy and aspirations is ostensibly, and seductively, colour-blind, operating as an apparently positive screen to mobilise achievement. That is, aspirations are deemed to be the cause of high achievement for some students, thus responsibility for not achieving high academic results, and for not raising the educational standards of the entire system, lies with families and students who have low or no aspirations. Aspirations constitute all students in the same way despite extensive evidence in the UK showing that all students do not achieve the same outcomes, that black African, black Caribbean, Pakistani, and Bangaldeshi students are likely to be unrepresented in the top tier of exam results (Gillborn 2010a). Furthermore, aspirations fail to explain why some students such as middle-class black and Bangladeshi students do not achieve similar results to white, middle-class students, even when they have the supposed same level of educational aspirations (Gillborn 2010a).

Nonetheless, white teachers and administrators in Poplar schools mobilise what they deem to be the acceptable and intelligible discourses of hard work, educational achievement, and mobility. This comprises a social justice project within the neoliberal ideal of constituting the legitimate entrepreneurial subject as white and middle class. If successfully attained this subjectivity will underscore the legitimacy of a politics of aspiration.

GEOGRAPHICAL IMAGINARIES AND POLICY ASPIRATIONS

> It is perfectly possible to argue that some distinctive objects are made of the mind, and that these objects, while appearing to exist objectively, have a fictional reality. . . . In other words, this universal practice of designating in one's mind a familiar space which is 'ours' and an unfamiliar space beyond 'ours' which is 'theirs' is a way of making geographical distinctions that *can be* entirely arbitrary. (Said 1978: 54, original emphasis)

The idea of an 'imaginative geography' and the manifestation of a 'fictional reality' provide an interesting way of thinking about the spatialities of difference. My concluding thoughts in this chapter build on the ways in which working-class schools and places are constructed as shameful and demonised. These are no-go areas in the eyes of the middle class (Lucey and Reay 2002, Reay 2007, Reay et al. 2007). What I want to examine is how other non-demonised places, in this case Canary Wharf, operate as imagined geographies important to schooling in Poplar. This includes the role companies such as Citigroup play in schools, and Canary Wharf as an embodiment of aspiration. Ms Kewell mused:

there's no reason if they're given the background these [Poplar students] cannot become our employees and our customers and our clients . . . there's no reason why they just can't rise above [the class system] if given the proper kind of background and education. (Ms Kewell, Citigroup)

The presence of Canary Wharf provides the representation of intended aspiration and achievement, a constant physical presence positioning successive generations of students. Ms Talon claimed that:

[o]ur kids now see Canary Wharf as an opportunity, but in some areas like Poplar I don't think they think of it as realistic yet that they can actually aspire to hold one of those high flying paid jobs up there . . . [B]ecause it's a generation thing isn't it? Each one becomes more able to see themselves . . . being able to take opportunities that present [themselves]. (Ms Talon, *Excellence in Cities*)

Canary Wharf does indeed provide an embodiment and horizon of possible employment that is otherwise absent in a highly parochial job market in Poplar (Hall 2007). Students can observe all thirty stories of offices: from their school yards, street corners, and the windows of their homes. Furthermore, Canary Wharf as an imaginary geography plays into what is seen as desirable and desiring educational subjectivities. Canary Wharf operates as 'a psychical investment in aspiration' in conjunction with the 'fantastical, imaginary projections built into policies' (J. Ringrose, personal correspondence, 2009).

This imaginary geography comprises how teachers, in reference to a place like Canary Wharf, can buy into the idea of aspirations as central to educational achievement; to urge students to try harder, with role models to show the way, and so forth. In Tower Hamlets the politics of aspiration could be seen to be successful in raising standards. There was significant improvement in the percentage of pupils achieving five or more General Certificate of Secondary Education subjects (GCSEs) at grade A*-C, which are examinations that complete the first stage of secondary school. A*-C is the highest band. In 1997 26 percent of students received five or more GCSEs; in 2001, 35 percent; in 2002, 44 percent: and in 2005 at the termination of the Poplar Action Zone, 51 percent (Tower Hamlets Council 2004, 2006). However, what is also noteworthy is whether aspirations are realised or not appears unimportant *relative* to the overall policy goal of raising educational standards. What is paramount for the state is that students are focused on this goal, that they adopt the requisite neoliberal 'repertoires of self' (O'Flynn and Petersen 2007).

Additionally, if considered within performance targets regarding educational achievement, and a name and shame culture attached to schools and places, then students are encouraged to think of other places aside from

Poplar, to deny in part the capacity to make place in Poplar. For, despite being an area of London that represents the complexity of immigration and white claims to nationhood, I suggest the urban imaginary put forward for students in Poplar is one of middle-class whiteness, constituted as central to academic achievement in the post-industrial city. The city is being re-imagined as places, or in the case of East London, a place, in which students can be displaced, and reinserted, renewed, and renovated. This is the paradox of area-based initiatives such as *Excellence in Cities*. One policy aim is to invest in neighbourhoods and people, to encourage people to make place. Another is about mobility and aspirations as escape; that is, aspirations imagine a geography anew *somewhere else.*

6 Parental Choice, the Multicultural City, and Whiteness in East Vancouver

> [I]n the past, I think we've tried to—I'll be overstating the case a bit by using this term, but we tried to protect schools. So whenever a school starts to have a bad reputation, when the families want to leave, we've tried to protect it by putting in supports and resources, but also by not letting the neighbouring schools take all the kids .... The legislation now doesn't give us any ground to say no, if there's space. (Senior administrator, Vancouver School Board, 2008)

Changes in 2001 to Section 74.1 of the British Columbia *School Act* (British Columbia Ministry of Education 1996 (2001)) allowed students to attend public schools outside of school attendance boundaries, or catchment areas, set by school boards. Public schools must now accept all students, if there is space, though students inside catchment areas continue to be guaranteed enrolment. This open enrolment policy overlapped with many Vancouver School Board (VSB) policies which had long supported choice in some form, including a cross-boundary policy developed in 1989 (VSB 1989 (Revised March 3 2003)).

In this chapter I explore the operation of choice within the multicultural, inner-city neighbourhood of Grandview Woodlands in East Vancouver, close to the Central Business District. I focus on the complex ways white, middle-class parents from one elementary school, Queen Victoria Annex, make sense of choice in relation to both elementary schooling[1] and where to live. To do this, I examine how the discourses of gentrification, multiculturalism, and the urban edge are drawn upon by white, middle-class parents to explain residential choices. I then connect these explanations of residential choice with choice of schools. In the latter, race and reputation coalesce to underpin white parents' decisions to send their children to schools other than those they deem as 'unsafe' or 'unsuitable'. I contend that school choice inscribes whiteness in East Vancouver, a contention that highlights the problematic discourses of multiculturalism, especially in relation to a white imaginary of the city and the nation.

URBAN IMAGINARIES: GENTRIFICATION, MULTICULTURALISM, AND THE URBAN EDGE

> "If you're looking for a manicured mega mall, Commercial Drive is not for you. If you're looking for funky, ethnic, hip stuff, it's probably just the place." (BC Passport 2009)

"[On Commercial Drive] [l]ess yuppies would be awesome. Also less crackheads." (Respondent #424 in Mosca and Spicer 2008: 52)

Vancouver has become increasingly gentrified over the past twenty to thirty years (Ley 1996), through a combination of individual residents renovating heritage homes and new apartment construction (Walks and Maaranen 2008). Gentrification has been uneven across the city, with less occurring in eastern neighbourhoods, such as Grandview Woodlands. This neighbourhood runs from the waterfront at Burrard Inlet south to the main east-west thoroughfare of Broadway, and from Clark Drive east to Nanimo Street (see Figure 6.1). The main north-south shopping street, Commercial Drive, is renowned for its 'alternative shops', 'ethnic' cafes and restaurants, along with homelessness and drug use. Grandview Woodlands has mixed land use: social and co-operative housing; apartments and heritage homes; and commercial and industrial areas (Tupechka et al. 1997). This combination of industrial land use, social housing and a generally 'progressive' political culture makes Grandview Woodlands 'a less-than-perfect nesting area for some gentrifiers' (Ley and Dobson 2008: 2494). Now, my interest is not in whether gentrification is or is not occurring in Grandview Woodlands. Rather I aim to explore how white, middle-class parents draw on discourses of gentrification, multiculturalism, and an urban edge to make sense of their choice to live in Grandview Woodlands.

A white, middle-class Queen Victoria Annex parent, Abigail, lamented the slow rate of change in the neighbourhood. Having been in Grandview Woodlands for thirteen years, Abigail displayed the tendencies of a 'pioneer gentrifier' (Lees et al. 2008), trying to anticipate the wave of change, and hoping to see the area gentrify in a similar manner to another Vancouver neighbourhood, Kitsilano.

> Going back sort of thirteen years or so ago, we rented in Kits[ilano] and this was before Kits became [gentrified]. . . . And so when we looked at buying in where we are now, we thought that Commercial Drive would kind of go that route over time and it's been very slow in doing that. . . . [T]here's been little changes, but it's been slow, slower than I thought it would be. But that's kind of what drove us to that neighbourhood here. (Abigail, Queen Victoria)

In the geographical imaginary of Vancouver, the west side is the area of sophisticated urbanism, and the east side is culturally 'authentic'. The east side is also redolent with danger, crime, and drugs (cf. Leonardo and Hunter 2007). For some parents, the reputation of East Vancouver and specifically Commercial Drive is its attraction, along with the onset of gentrification. Sharon, a white Queen Victoria parent noted:

> the neighbourhood is definitely being gentrified, and I think those [changes] are good things. . . . It is always changing. . . . There's always new shops, things closing down, other ones opening up, but it has

always maintained its edginess. It never really goes away, and sometimes there's even a nastiness out there. . . . Maybe that's what makes it
unique, is just that whole other side, right? (Sharon, Queen Victoria)

That the character of the neighbourhood can change, while retaining some
sort of place integrity, is reflected in a local newsletter produced by a real
estate agent. The newsletter identifies the different types of shops being
introduced along Commercial Drive, and states:

> [s]o you're thinking: Gentrification! There goes the Drive. . . . But in
> fact Grandview is evolving back into something it always was: a place
> for families. . . . So yes, the Drive is changing. Still funky, less gritty.
> But it's hard to argue against people who are helping to save the re-
> maining heritage of the neighbourhood, adding some infill, patronizing
> the local businesses and making the sincerest form of commitment to
> community: they're going to raise their kids here. (Price 2005)

This idea of investment in neighbourhood is an important one for understanding why it is possible to defend and even advocate urban change
marked as gentrification (see Byrne 2003). This is partly connected to
the emancipatory thesis of gentrification. New middle classes with more
'progressive' politics, especially in Canadian cities (Ley 1996), may generate new forms of social milieu in cities. These middle classes are driven
by a desire to transform an area by working with, rather than displacing,
existing residents (Lees et al. 2008: 213–215). Some of the parents at
Queen Victoria saw themselves in this regard, recognising that when they
arrived in the area, most no more than twelve years earlier, they too might
have been considered gentrifiers. However, it was their adherence to what
these parents believed to be the social authenticity and multicultural ethic
of the area that ameliorated any negative charge of gentrification. Nonetheless, for some, the charge of gentrification continues, along with the
pejorative aspect of displacement. Therefore, rather than see themselves
as gentrifiers, these parents preferred to recast aspects of gentrification as
urban renewal.[2]

> It's not gentrification. I see it more as urban renewal . . . So as prices
> have gone up, you do tend to get, you know, pressure to build [con-
> dominiums] . . . And so the neighbourhood is changing in that we're
> seeing a lot of . . . traditional core businesses being forced out by rents.
> There's . . . resentment about that . . . people tend to link it to families
> coming here and buying houses, and the houses cost a lot of money.
> So there's a kind of . . . resentment against the businesses being forced
> out, and then you see young families coming in and spending stupefy-
> ing amounts of money. People are making the wrong connection. They
> think it's a gentrification. I don't . . . I would say the process . . . [is]

urban renewal. Gentrification is a very poor name for it. Now it has this label of gentrification. (John, Queen Victoria)

Even in denial the 'pioneer gentrifier' commits to a new urbane ethic, yet also breaks the ground for further gentrification (Lees et al. 2008). The more that moving to a multicultural and economically diverse neighbourhood becomes the 'right' choice for white, middle-class parents, the easier it is for other white, middle-class parents to follow. In relation to forms of 'social' gentrification where middle-class people buy and renovate existing housing stock, 'the creation of mixed class communities in which people are choosing to live in close spatial (if not social) proximity to other groups gives rise to the need to understand what the ties of space are and how identities are constructed' (Butler and Robson 2003: 18). In this part of Vancouver these ties are intimately connected to the complexity of white parents' commitments to multiculturalism.

Ambivalent Commitments to Multiculturalism

I think it's a very culturally and racially diverse neighbourhood. It's very diverse as far as a socio-economic background. I think it's a fabulous neighbourhood. It's very interesting. There's lots to do. There's lots of parks. . . . Commercial Drive is really a dynamic neighbourhood as far as shops and restaurants and the opportunities for families and it's—yeah, it's just a funky East Van neighbourhood. (Gillian, Queen Victoria)

Well, there's never a dull moment in the Commercial Drive area. I think . . . some of my friends think, you know, when I moved here in 1988, 'What on earth are you doing moving to that neighbourhood? It's full of crime, it's full of drugs. . . .' And it is. There is a lot of that, but there's a lot of really good stuff too. . . . I think it's sort of like this little Bohemian spot. People like to come here for the music, the cafes, the great coffee shops, the diverse ethnic groupings. . . . [T]here's Ethiopian restaurants. There are fabulous Italian restaurants. There are great sushi spots. . . . You can just get any kind of food, really, along that strip. (Sharon, Queen Victoria)

For some Queen Victoria parents, 'ethnic diversity' is an attractive facet of living in Grandview Woodlands. Additionally, when these parents talk about schooling in this area of Vancouver they tend to reinforce the connection to neighbourhood, the role of the school, and the significance of difference and diversity; that 'multiculturalism is seen as an important value reflecting inclusivity in a diverse, global world' (Reay et al. 2007: 1044). Denise, a white, working class parent, for example, identified the importance of her children interacting with a wide range of people.

> [It's] very important, very, very important, because they need to know that there's other things going on in the world and their little privilege is not the way that it is everywhere. So, it is very important that there are kids with special needs and Native kids and whatever. . . . I think it's really important. I don't like the idea of everything being white and privileged . . . because it's not like that in life. I think it's very important. (Denise, Queen Victoria)

This commitment to educating children in what is considered to be a multicultural neighbourhood does not necessarily lead, for some parents, to the outcomes that Denise desires. As Reay (2008) points out, what often occurs is a *'social mix with little social mixing'* (p. 92, my emphasis). Peter seemed to indicate this outcome.

> My kids' friends—my kids' friends typically will have parents that are about the same age and demographic as we are. . . . [S]ome of us were talking about that. I mean . . . that was never a conscious thing . . . We [have] got a pretty white bunch of friends. . . . So I mean there are some—there are—there are some people—some immigrants or, you know, second-generation folks or whatever. But it's a pretty—pretty middle class, standard older Canadian bunch. Yeah, that's true. (Peter, Queen Victoria)

The white parents at Queen Victoria appear thoughtful and committed to a multicultural imaginary of the city. Nonetheless some of these parents seems to articulate a certain understanding of how multiculturalism operates in Vancouver. John identified that Vancouver's neighbourhoods and schools are perhaps simultaneously ethnically diverse and homogenous. He suggested that:

> it might be this issue of mobility that—you know, let's face it, the South Indian community is on the south slope, you know, Fraser . . . where I've also lived. And they live there and they go to those schools. There's the group around . . . Little Chinatown at 41st and Victoria. And the schools there—if you go in the school there, they're almost 99 percent Chinese. . . . So, those groups are tending to stay in their neighbourhood because, shall we say, they want to be in that neighbourhood because it didn't happen by coincidence. I don't think so. And so they want that community feeling and the kids are all in schools in that community. So there is a—what would you call that? There is a kind of separation of communities in . . . [Vancouver] and it's this idea of multiculturalism mixes everyone and not really, no. (John, Queen Victoria)

As John notes, there are areas of Vancouver that are seen as having high proportions of certain ethnic groups, such as Chinese-speaking populations in the neighbourhoods of Marpole (36.4 percent in 2006) and Victoria-Fraserview (48.1 percent in 2006) (Statistics Canada 2008). However, there is a white imaginary at work in accounts like John's, in the ascription of racialised choices of residence to groups like Chinese Canadians and not to white people. While I do not want to give undue emphasis to demographic change, a notable change in Grandview Woodlands was the increase in non-visible minority residents, from 58 percent in 2001 to 62 percent in 2006, while the City of Vancouver remained steady at 49% over the same period. Statistics Canada defines 'visible minority' as:

> persons who are identified according to the Employment Equity Act as being non-Caucasian in race or non-white in colour. Under the Act, Aboriginal persons are not considered to be members of visible minority groups. (Statistics Canada 2010)

Therefore, leaving aside the problematic use of Caucasian in the above, in part Queen Victoria parents' investment in the multicultural ideal may gloss over the increasing whiteness in the area of Grandview Woodlands. Multiculturalism here operates at the level of national policy (Mackey 1999) and city actuality, but the demographic representation of diversity does not deal with the nuances of interaction, and the ways in which choice is layered on top of commitments to difference. What is absent from the discourses of multiculturalism drawn upon by some of the Queen Victoria parents is that apparently white people do not need to integrate in the inner city. In the prevailing discourses of liberal multiculturalism, white people would never overtly choose to live with other white people, but this inadvertently happens as people choose residences for other characteristics ('safe', 'convenient', etc.) that elide the geographies of race (Delaney 2002). Similar discourses circulate in relation to place, policy, and school choice in Grandview Woodlands.

PLACE, POLICY, AND CHOICE

Despite the existence of both provincial and school board policies on open enrolment, the VSB continues to encourage parents to send their children to the nearest or 'neighbourhood' school, as designated by the VSB catchment areas. The VSB considers that 'it is important to maintain the relationship between residential location and school catchment areas' (VSB 1989 (Revised 2003)). The idea of public schools being a crucial part of a neighbourhood is stated by a senior administrator with the VSB.

> [S]chools are a very essential part of the fabric of the community. . . . [T]here is an attachment in the way that there isn't to other institutions. I mean, it draws people in, as a public institution. It puts people together that might not otherwise have been together, so it

has . . . a real role in terms of almost creating community. (Senior administrator, VSB)

Nonetheless, school choice works to displace the local school and constitutes this cultural institution as merely one of a range of consumptive choices, which may or may not impinge on whether parents decide to remain in a neighbourhood.

> So the jury's still out whether it's the right neighbourhood as far as I'm concerned for kids. . . . Because one of the things that I keep struggling with, is whether I should send her to private school. You know, it's a lot cheaper to send her to private school than it is to sell my house and buy a house on the west side. So that's kind of where I'm at. (Abigail, parent, Queen Victoria)

For other parents at Queen Victoria, there is no such opportunity cost in play. They have a stated commitment to schooling in Grandview Woodlands which is associated with place making, neighbourhood, and the role of the school. These parents tended to have resided in the area for approximately ten years, and lived in or a few blocks outside of the Queen Victoria catchment area.

> Why would you move to a neighbourhood if you're not going to make any connection in your neighbourhood? . . . Why would they be here? . . . I know there's a girl down the street who sends her . . . [son] over to the West Side, and I don't really know why. I think maybe because he went to preschool there, and they developed relationships there. . . . But I don't think those people will stay in the neighbourhood, because they're not invested. . . . They're here to flip their house in two years and move back to the West Side. (Sharon, Queen Victoria)

> I think there's a detriment when . . . people in neighbourhoods decide they're going to like send their kid to some other school completely across town . . . I mean I feel mixed. . . . I think it's good that there is some choice. But I think that ultimately, you know, whatever—but the school is never going to be perfect, like nothing—nothing is. . . . You have to make a commitment to, you know, taking the good with the bad and try and make a change. (Gillian, Queen Victoria)

Additionally, this connection to neighbourhood reinforces and complicates multiple policy articulations of place: the definition of the Grandview Woodlands neighbourhood according to the City of Vancouver; the VSB school catchment areas; and the open enrolment policies of the province and the VSB.

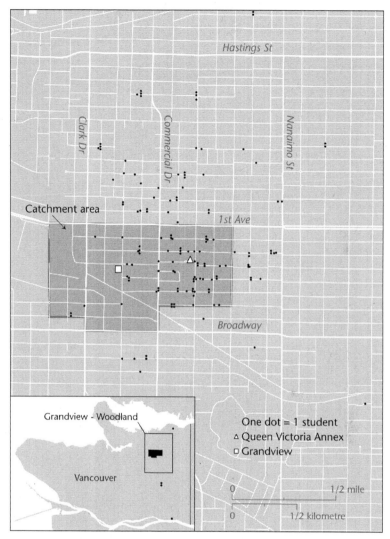

Figure 6.1 The catchment area for Queen Victoria Annex and Grandview Elementary. It shows the approximate residential location of all Queen Victoria students. It accurately represents the numbers of students inside and outside the catchment area. Map: Eric Leinberger (2009).

The cartographic imagination of a catchment area generates an idea of place as a set of coordinates, or something to be mapped. Figure 6.1, another cartographic representation, shows that just over 50 percent (73 out of 144) of students live *outside* of the Queen Victoria Annex catchment area. Catchment areas thus continue as a centralising modality, as a governmental intervention into the city, that is simultaneously circumvented by policies on open enrolment. This capacity for mobility is then complicated by the City of Vancouver's definition of the Grandview Woodlands neighbourhood. Parents can think of Queen Victoria as their neighbourhood school even when they are outside the catchment area. This disjuncture between what is represented by the catchment area and the practices of parental choice was pointed to by Ms Mitchell, an administrator at Queen Victoria.

> If you look at our [student] numbers . . . [the VSB] claim[s] that less than half our school actually lives within our catchment area. But . . . it's a very small catchment area and there's actually quite a bubble around us, where we are the closest school. . . . I think it's a real neighbourhood hub and that the people that are choosing to come here are choosing to come here because this is where the kid's friends go. . . . I don't see many people driving across town to get here. . . . My sense is that people really do live quite close to our school and want to come here. (Ms Mitchell, Queen Victoria)

This suggests a distinction between policy-defined neighbourhood and neighbour-defined neighbourhood, that the two do not necessarily coincide. What is clear from the way parents and administrators talk about both the area of Grandview Woodlands and Queen Victoria Annex is that they constitute place as contested and fluid (McDowell 1999, Massey 2005). What defines these places are not only maps, but socio-spatial practices of choice. In this regard:

> [p]laces are made through power relations which construct the rules which define boundaries. These boundaries are both social and spatial—they define who belongs to a place and who may be excluded, as well as the location or site of the experience. (McDowell 1999: 4)

What is of further interest to me is how people make sense of choices of schools and places of residence; specifically the ways neighbourhood and school boundaries and differences are articulated, defended, and transgressed in this area of Vancouver.

Choice, Reputation, and Being 'Too Aboriginal'

An extensive array of research has identified the multiple ways parents select schools for their children, including on the basis of school reputations (e.g., Ball 2003, Campbell et al. 2009, Levine-Rasky 2008). Information generated by governments or educational think tanks, or what Ball (2003) terms formal or 'cold knowledge' (p. 100), may improve or diminish school reputations. In Vancouver, a free-market think tank, the Fraser Institute, publishes yearly league tables, circulated in a province-wide newspaper. These tables rank all elementary and secondary schools in British Columbia with elite private schools repeatedly topping of the list. Concomitantly, informal information, or what Ball (2003) terms 'hot knowledge' (p. 100), circulates between family, friends, and neighbours and plays a role in how parents compare and choose schools. An administrator at Queen Alexandria Elementary, adjacent to the Queen Victoria catchment area, noted:

> there's certainly . . . in people's minds, there are schools of choice even within the inner city, and I think word of mouth about various schools and what they're doing. . . . And I think . . . unfortunately . . . some families that may have preconceived notions about a school. And so then they may try to get a child across boundary into one of the other schools. . . . And that's going to be true in any neighbourhood you're in. You hear something from a neighbour about one school and you think, 'Oh, I would like my child in the other school,' as a result. And that could be word of mouth based on experience ten years before that has no bearing on the school or the community at that point. (Administrator, Queen Alexandria)

Schools in East Vancouver, and particularly Grandview Woodlands, have poor reputations (Ley and Dobson 2008). These schools are thus also implicated in the geographical imaginary that divides the city into west and east down the dividing north-south corridor of Main Street. Additionally, school reputations play a role *within* Grandview Woodlands.

Queen Victoria Annex (K–5) and Grandview Elementary (K–7) share the same catchment area, and are less than a kilometre apart (see Figure 6.1). Queen Victoria was built as an annex to the Grandview school in 1963, and comes under the supervision of the Principal of Grandview, with a Vice Principal responsible for the day-to-day running of the Annex (Lee and MacFarlan 2001). Grandview is a designated 'inner city school', and thus receives extra resourcing, including support staff and a full-time kindergarten/day care. Queen Victoria receives a portion of these additional resources.[3]

The common arrangement in the Vancouver school district is that an annex (usually K–3) is the feeder school for an elementary school. However, Victoria Annex virtually operates as an independent school, and few if any students move from Queen Victoria to Grandview at the end their schooling at Queen Victoria. Ms Mitchell outlined that at the end of the 2007/2008 school year:

> there . . . was one student that went to Grandview. So it's not a choice that [Queen Victoria parents] make to go to Grandview . . . Grandview

doesn't have a great reputation . . . there seems to be a stigma out there around Grandview School. (Ms Mitchell, Queen Victoria)

The reasons for this reputation vary. There is the cold knowledge of being ranked 916th out of 981 elementary schools in British Columbia in the Fraser Institute league tables. This information clearly does not work in favour of attracting parents to Grandview Elementary and could to some extent explain antipathy to this school.

However, what seems more critical in explaining white, middle-class parents' antipathy to Grandview school is unfavourable 'hot knowledge' about the school's Aboriginal students and Aboriginal focus. Prior to World War I, predominantly white students attended Grandview. In the 1960s, it was seen as one of the best schools in Vancouver, where the children of prominent business and professional citizens were educated (Greyell 2001, Lee and MacFarlan 2001). By 2006/2007, the demographics of the city and the school had changed. Grandview enrols 101 Aboriginal students, or 54 percent, significantly more than the VSB average and the province average (see Figure 6.2). Since 1991, the school has an Aboriginal name, the full name of the school being Grandview/ ʔuukinak'Uuh (a Nu-chah-nulth word meaning 'grand view'), and the outside and inside of the school are resplendent with Aboriginal artwork and symbols.

Open enrolment enables Aboriginal parents to select Grandview as a desirable school for their child. A white administrator at Grandview, Ms

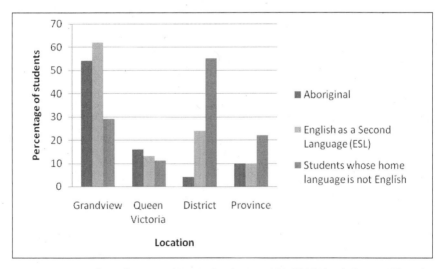

Figure 6.2 Student demographics (school year 2006/2007) of Queen Victoria, Grandview, Vancouver School District, and Province of British Columbia. Adapted from School Data Summary Grandview and Queen Victoria 2002/2003–2006/2007 (British Columbia Ministry of Education 2008).

Sedin, reflected that for Aboriginal parents the school is 'a comfortable place for those families to be. So . . . for that inner city, poor socioeconomic group, this is a wonderful haven'. Yet while Grandview has an excellent reputation for supporting Aboriginal students, with many innovative programmes, there are market implications for this all too rare occurrence in public schooling.

> Not in the picture. . . . *It's not our demographic.* . . . I think it's that [Grandview] seems to be geared towards the Native population, First Nations people, and . . . they're filling needs that that community needs, but *it's not my community.* So, that wouldn't be a pick for us. (Sharon, Queen Victoria, my emphasis)

> Grandview has quite a lot of, shall we say, problems. And some parents . . . they'll live within a block of Grandview but they'll come to Queen Vic because . . . the parents feel they're refugees from Grandview because over the years there have been a number of social problems and other issues at Grandview. . . . [Grandview's] a good school as far as I know. But that's—I find it kind of startling that people who live beside Grandview would walk their kids over here. . . . And I haven't really heard of any like dire problems. But . . . I know from one of the people that lives there and walks his kids over here . . . that he just felt the atmosphere was not good. . . . *So it's the social—I don't know if you call it a rumour. There's . . . just a feeling that parents have that some of the things that happened there were dangerous for their kids.* (John, Queen Victoria, my emphasis)

Discourses of danger, reputations, and risks circulate to constitute Grandview as an unacceptable present and already rejected future schooling option for most parents at Queen Victoria Annex. Ms Sedin noted that for some non-Aboriginal parents there:

> is a little bit too much of an Aboriginal tone to [Grandview school]. . . . I think where choice killed [this] school is there are Aboriginal kids all around [Vancouver] who aren't functioning in their own school and somebody tells the parents, 'Why don't you go to Grandview? It's an Aboriginal school'. The students [ask] me, 'Is this an Aboriginal school?' I say 'well no, it's a public school of the Vancouver School system that happens to have a large percentage of our students of Aboriginal heritage'. (Ms Sedin, Grandview)

This is the problem of recuperating race, for while race can generate solidarity it also draws on and is constituted by racism (Gilroy 2000). It is not whether Grandview is successful in educating Aboriginal students that matters in this market, it becomes about Aboriginality as visible, or being *too* Aboriginal. Ms Sedin noted:

families who are . . . interested in a gentrified lifestyle they're . . . exercising their option to not come [to Grandview], but to apply to go [to Victoria Annex]. . . . [C]hoice, is working here . . . I think young parents are quite leery of—well they want to make sure that the children are going to get a [certain type of] education and be with sort of like-minded kind of adults. (Ms Sedin, Grandview)

There appears to be a complex three-way struggle over the right to belong in settler cities like Vancouver; between Aboriginal peoples, those who collectively assert 'settler' status (usually constituted as white), and immigrants, usually marked as non-white 'ethnics' (Anderson 2000). This struggle can play out in the often mundane practices of school choice that pertain to the differentiation of difference. Specifically, white parents grapple with defining an acceptable level of exposure to difference for their children when it comes to them attending schools, as opposed to merely residing in an inner city multicultural neighbourhood. This is the threat of difference, especially when concretised as race in the practices of schooling futures and success (cf. Reay 2008, Reay et al. 2007).

'FINE-TUNING' WHITENESS

Aside from being an alternative to Grandview Elementary, white middle-class parents send their children to Queen Victoria for many reasons, including: one, it is a small school where teachers 'know all names of the students'; two, Queen Victoria is the 'local' school either due to, or despite, what the catchment boundaries indicate; three, access to all-day kindergarten, which is highly prized in a city where child care is limited; and four, and the reason on which I focus here, Queen Victoria is a desirable school that provides an 'acceptable' schooling option in this part of a multicultural city.

Queen Victoria has a significantly different student demographic than not only Grandview but also the Vancouver school district as a whole. Ethnicity data about schools in Vancouver tends to be presented either according to student language use, or identifying students as Aboriginal/non-Aboriginal. As Figure 6.2 shows, out of 133 students enrolled in the 2006/2007 school year, Queen Victoria Annex had far lower percentages of students who are English as a Second Language (ESL) (13 percent) or whose home language is not English (11 percent), than the VSB average (24 percent and 55 percent, respectively), and Grandview (62 percent and 29 percent, respectively). Queen Victoria had a higher than average percentage of Aboriginal students than the district, 16 percent or 21 students, but this was much lower than the 54 percent at Grandview.

Queen Victoria does have higher number of students who are not categorised as either of the two language categories ESL and non-English speaking at home. These uncategorised student numbers increased at Queen Victoria from 68 percent in 2003/2004 to 74 percent in 2007/2008 (British Columbia Ministry of Education 2008). In other words, most students at Queen Victoria nominate English as their primary language. The relative usefulness of this language data in ascertaining whether these students would identify as white is diminished in a multigenerational, immigrant nation like Canada. It is also evident in the Grandview data that some ESL students must also identify or be identified as Aboriginal.

Nonetheless, despite this data being inconclusive about whether Queen Victoria is demographically becoming a white school or not, there is clearly something distinct about this school, relating to the lack of diversity on language lines, especially when compared to both Grandview and the Vancouver school district (Yoon and Gulson 2010). White parents and Ms Mitchell noted this relative lack of what they deemed to be ethnic diversity.

> We're about ten percent First Nations and we have a few, probably about the same percentage Asian, I guess and then we're probably seventy to seventy five percent somewhere, in the Caucasian range. Which is . . . [a] huge anomaly for the city of Vancouver. (Ms Mitchell, Queen Victoria)

> So you do have different groups [in the school] . . . . But in terms of First Nations or the Chinese community, actually there seem to be fewer kids now if you look at the school yearly photos. And I'm not quite sure why that is. *Maybe the school is too, um, fine-tuned.* (John, Queen Victoria, my emphasis)

> When I first went there, I thought this was going to be a great sort of diverse school . . . and it's not . . . going to be a stratified school where my daughter is with all the kids . . . that are all looking just like her. But, in fact, if I'm honest, when I look around her classroom, it turns out they kind of are. Like I mean, there's a few kids from different cultures or backgrounds, but actually not that many . . . compared to Vancouver. . . . I can honestly say that it didn't occur to me that I was putting my kid into what some people could call a 'white flight school' . . . or something like that. I did make a conscious decision [that] I didn't want her in the only school where she wouldn't be an immigrant. . . . I have no problem admitting that. (Peter, Queen Victoria)

While identifying the apparent dominance of white students, parents resist the idea that the school be characterised as a 'white flight school'. This is, of course, an understandable position for these parents who consider choice of schooling as complementary to their commitment to engage with, not distance themselves from, the inner city and all its complexities, dangers, and opportunities. Nonetheless, the tensions between choosing a school and residence are clear. For example, Peter wanted a diverse school for his daughter; while at the same time being concerned that she would be the only one who 'wouldn't be an immigrant'. This is presumably immigrant as non-white, the 'other' in the nation and the city (Hage 1998, Hesse 1997, Razack 2002).

This idea of choosing schools in order to be around diversity but not too much diversity, is something that another parent, Sharon, also attributed to non-white parents.

> *Interviewer:* How do you think factors like race and class . . ., how do they impact people's decisions in what school to send people to, their children to?
> *Sharon:* Do I have to be politically correct in answering this?

> *Interviewer:* No, no.
> *Sharon:* Well, I think that there are certain schools are known as, you know, that one is a Native school. That one is a Chinese school. That one is a whatever school. People who lived in the neighbourhood, they figured that out for themselves, and they figured out where they slot in.

> *Interviewer:* So, it is a pretty key factor in school choice?
> *Sharon:* Yeah . . . [And at Queen Victoria] Well, I do think we have one of everybody in our school. I think it's predominantly white. It seems to be the white Anglo Saxon parents choose that school, for whatever reasons. Like I was telling you, Lord Beaconsfield had a high Asian population just because that seems to be an Asian neighbourhood, right. (Sharon, Queen Victoria)

I am interested in the ascription of racialised choice for non-whites ('Asians', 'Chinese', 'Natives'), while whites choose 'for whatever reasons'. As Gillborn (2008) contends, '[a] central characteristic of Whiteness is a process of "naturalisation" such that White becomes the norm from which other "races" stand apart and in relation to which they are defined' (p. 169). White parents seem to have no trouble identifying race as a factor when 'other people' choose schools. However, white parents seem to both recognise whiteness while attempting to disavow it.

Davies and Aurini (2008) propose that the practices of 'concerted cultivation' underpin parental choice of schools in Canada. A 'good' parent actively assesses the schooling options for their child, as part of a suite of activities aimed at managing their child's educational career. One aspect of this concerted cultivation is the rationalisation of supporting choice on the basis of parental responsibility. If the range of schooling options is unequal, this is a problem for policy makers not parents. Parents who participate in the education market are acting as any responsible parent should. While Davies and Aurini are mostly concerned with class, I think this idea of responsible parenting also relates to an eliding of race and racism in Grandview Woodland.

> I'm not going to say that I think race is a factor. . . . I don't think there are that many people that are—well, maybe this is naïve—but I don't think there are that many people that are genuinely racist, insofar as they think, 'I don't want my kid with a kid of another race.' People, I think, just—like nobody I know is like that. Nobody I know is like that. You know what I mean? . . . But I think there are people that worry that if their kid is in a class that's predominantly full of kids that don't speak English, then they're worried, rightfully I think, that their kid isn't going to get equal treatment . . . or as good a treatment as he can get somewhere else. . . . So I think that sometimes school choice does some de facto ethnic stratification. And I don't believe it's because people are racist. I think it's just a fact of life. (Peter, Queen Victoria).

> I guess, you know, quite honestly, if Grandview was my only choice, I probably would have been more pressed to make a decision of either a west side or a private school, in the sense that I am a strong believer in that who you surround yourself with, will determine the kind of expectations you have on yourself. And I realise that there's some arguments that can be made there, but, you know, I'm of the high achieving route, I want my daughter to be a high achiever. I want her to go to university, you know, and I think that if you surround yourself with like minded parents, like minded kids, then you improve the odds of that happening. (Abigail, Queen Victoria)

These examples represent the complexity of navigating difference where it is most pronounced in inner city schooling and the inner city, and the way choice rationalities elide other pernicious aspects of markets. On the one hand, the ideas of being naïve or rejecting Grandview because too many Aboriginal students will hold a non-Aborignal child back from educational achievement and future success, these ideas embody the middle-class dilemma. That is, what is 'good' for a middle-class child may often contrast with liberal sensibilities. This represents the elusive nature regarding what the middle classes value, where '[i]impersonal values and principles are hard things to pin down when it comes to making difficult decisions and can very quickly become sidelined when set over and against other values embedded in putting family first' (Ball 2003: 123). On the other hand, whiteness works to naturalise racism which is glossed over by concerns for children, responsible parenting, and so forth. Supposedly, in the cultural practices of choice, only non-whites, such as Chinese parents or First Nations parents, make racialised decisions in choosing schools.

SCHOOL CHOICE, CONSUMING MULTICULTURALISM, AND THE WHITE NATION

> I mean . . . from listening to other people talk in [Grandview Woodlands], I certainly heard that perception that, 'Oh, yeah, I might buy a house in this neighbourhood and live here but I would never send my kid to an east side school'. (Gillian, Queen Victoria parent)

> Across the globe, citizens of the metropolis are asking themselves 'how do we live with difference?', as the problem of multiculturalism poses a challenge to the way in which people make sense of their own lives. (Keith 2005: 38)

White, middle-class parents choose to live in a neighbourhood like Grandview Woodlands partly through a commitment to a multicultural ideal that is both abstract and realised. In Canada, multiculturalism is underpinned by relations between a dominant national culture equated with British (white) Canadians and 'others', who are to be valued for their contributions in reinforcing the national norms (Mackey 1999). Moreover, multiculturalism is safely consumed (Keith 2005) if certain representations of it such as restaurants and exotic shops are endorsed as supplementing not supplanting national culture.

However, while multiculturalism in multiple forms is to be navigated in East Vancouver, Aboriginal peoples, or more precisely students, pose a seemingly intractable challenge to multiculturalism in Grandview Woodlands. This resonates with a tendency in settler nations to treat 'white-Aboriginal' and 'Anglo-ethnic' relations (Hage 1998) as discrete from other forms of interrelations. That is, 'the Whites relating to Aboriginal people appear as totally unaffected by multiculturalism, while the "Anglos" relating to "ethnics" appear as if they have no Aboriginal question about which to worry' (Hage 1998: 24).

Furthermore, what is desirable in a neighbourhood can be a problem in schooling. Thus, white Queen Victoria parents in a marketised educational environment take up a particular form of the neoliberal entrepreneur. This is tied up with ideas of parental responsibility which understandably become accentuated within marketised policy realms like schooling, where individuals are responsible for both success and failure (Brown 2003). White, middle-class parents in Grandview Woodlands are safe in the knowledge that, through school choice, they do not likely need to send their children to the local school if its edginess entails risk, or exceeds acceptability (i.e., too many ESL students or Aboriginal students). As such, these parents retain the choice to be part of a neighbourhood and not part of certain schools. As Reay et al. (2007) note: 'The ability to move in and out of spaces marked as "other" becomes part of the process through which this particular fraction of the white middle classes come to know themselves as both privileged and dominant' (p. 1047). White parents are thus simultaneously quarantined from and constitutive of a politics of multicultural space.

In discussing multiculturalism from the view of 'white culture' in Australia, Hage (1998) notes that both white racists and white multiculturalists, who express support for multiculturalism, continue to undertake practices that draw on discourses of a '"White nation" fantasy' (p. 18). Hage argues that 'White multiculturalism works to mystify, and to keep out of public discourse, other multicultural realities in which White people are not the overwhelming occupiers of the centre of national space' (p. 19). A similar claim can be made about Canada and Vancouver. In the case of white parents in Grandview Woodlands, 'others' are important to constitute a multicultural Vancouver. Nevertheless, white parents retain the capacity as 'spatial managers' (Hage 1998) of the white nation fantasy as to adjudge whether other groups such as 'Chinese' or 'Indo-Canadians' are integrating in a satisfactory manner, and as to whether they, as white parents, will choose to participate in an inclusive, cultural transformation. Therefore, multiculturalism can manifest as whiteness, for non-white 'others' who choose schools and neighbourhoods are always already marked by claims of failing to integrate.

7 Racial Neoliberalism, Education Policy, and the City

> [The city] was like a deranged experiment in social Darwinism, designed by a bored researcher who kept one thumb permanently on the fast-forward button. (Gibson 1984: 14)

This book has explored the myriad ways neoliberal education policy, broadly conceived, comes to be constitutive and indicative of contemporary inner city areas in Sydney, London, and Vancouver. In taking the approach of a policy theorist, notably that the act of problematising is a politics (Ball 1995, Simons et al. 2009b), I aimed to deconstruct public policy discourses that account for the relationships between schooling and the city. I wanted to explore the complexity and messiness that comprises education policy processes and practices in inner city areas. In attempting to account for this complexity, this book is as much exploratory as it is definitive, for '[m]y work takes place between unfinished abutments and anticipatory strings of dots' (Foucault 1994b: 223). This final chapter is no different; it can be read as a coda to this book *and* as unfinished work.

This chapter briefly reviews the analytic scope of a spatial approach to educational policy studies. To do this, I draw together the conceptualisations employed in this book, notably governmentality, space, and place, with the empirical chapters on the processes and practices of K–12 education policy, pertaining to markets, in Sydney, London, and Vancouver. I then draw this book to a close by suggesting neoliberal education policy provides the conditions for increasingly and inexorably racialised inner city areas. Specifically, I utilise the notion of racial neoliberalism (Goldberg 2009), and emphasise the operation of personal preferences and privatised difference (Brown 2006) to understand the apparent invisibility of race in neoliberal education policy. I conclude that this invisibility implicates education policy as part of neoliberal racisms, both in the (re)inscription of white, middle-class imaginaries and in the generation of inner cities as racialised places.

SPACE, PLACE, AND POLICY

In this book I employed a spatial approach to education policy analysis. Spatial concepts can be stimuli 'for thinking creatively about movements between policies, processes, and instances of inclusion and exclusion in a fresh light, from different vantage points, to provide a counter-perspective of social life as a process of change' (Armstrong 2007: 108). More precisely, in this book I was interested in the analytic scope of relational notions of space and place, and the possibilities for thinking creatively about connections between policy, schooling, and the city in Sydney, London and Vancouver.

The policy foci in the preceding chapters illustrate the relatively straightforward point that neoliberal education policy is globalised (Rizvi and Lingard 2009), with similar policy ideas and enactments regarding markets and choice introduced in myriad countries and cities. However, the context in which neoliberal policy, such as school choice initiatives, is made and unfolds also matters (Taylor 2010). I was further interested in how education policy directions correspond with other policy realms in the city. In London, *Excellence in Cities* aimed to use education policy as a way of improving schooling, and parents' confidence in cities. The policy was intended to work in conjunction with other urban area-based initiatives, such as 'regeneration' strategies, to comprise 'joined-up' policy interventions into areas of 'deprivation' (Cochrane 2007). In Sydney, the restructuring of schooling associated with *Building the Future* was never explicitly considered part of other social and urban policy initiatives. Nevertheless, the Department of Education and Training implicitly connected education to the inner city by positing restructuring as a response to demographic shifts. Education policy was thus supplanted by policy-led urban change such as gentrification by capital, undertaken by state/corporate development projects.

In addition to connecting education policy to other urban realms, the educational policies examined in this book draw on, and invoke, a variety of spatial discourses. *Building the Future* was ostensibly introduced to revitalise declining inner city public schooling, a decline connected to changes in the inner city, including the increased provision of housing for single professional people or for couples with one or no children. *Excellence in Cities* was aimed at improving educational standards and creating aspirational pathways in deprived urban areas, including Tower Hamlets in East London. The legislation of open enrolment in British Columbia, with changes to the provincial *School Act*, and its introduction in Vancouver, constituted the possible movement of students across the city as a desirable and intended policy outcome. Each of these education policy directions depended on particular spatial mobilisations: the constitution of the city through demographics; the identification of disadvantage as bounded and located in place; and, the cartography, metaphor, and materiality of school choice that underpins remaining within and crossing catchment boundaries.

These spatial mobilisations also emphasise education policy and space as co-generative (Taylor 2009b, Thiem 2008). I was, and continue to be, interested in relational space, focusing on the interrelations of contingent and provisional subjectivities and entities, with relations identified as practices. From such a position, relational space is dependent on multiplicity, on an overlapping rather than conterminous heterogeneity (Massey 2005, Murdoch 2006). In this book, I accepted the theoretical invitation posed by relational space, following which I attempted to identify the connections between education policy and the programmes, rationalities, and technologies of governmentality. My focus then became the interplay of governmentality, neoliberal policy, and space.

Policy appears always implicated in the possibilities of space; policy repeatedly and insistently intervenes to make space. Policy thus not only unfolds in designated spaces but also constitutes 'those spaces as part of the governing activity' (Dikeç 2007: 280). This designation can include the boundaries of an area-based initiative; school catchment areas in a quasi-market; or the use of student enrolment numbers to denote failing schools in demographically designated, 'deprived' spaces requiring policy remediation. As Murdoch (2006) identifies, 'spaces are made of complex sets of relations so that any spatial "solidity" must be seen as an accomplishment, something that has to be achieved in the face of flux and instability' (p. 23). Policy comprises a spatial accomplishment to enable, though not determine, the take-up of desirable subjectivities; to 'elicit, promote, facilitate, foster and attribute various capacities, qualities and statuses to particular agents' (Dean 1999: 32). The take-up, or not, of these subjectivities is differentiated according to the specifics of how policy unfolds and where it unfolds.

In writing the above paragraph I am aware of how easily space and place become interchangeable categories. In this book I have tried to use them as related notions, but analytically distinct. I have understood place as an articulated moment in socio-spatial relations, as an event rather than merely represented cartographically or statistically (Massey 1993b, 2005). This accords credence to ideas of interaction, difference, and negotiation; places become, and are always becoming, *'moments of encounter'* (Amin and Thrift 2002: 30, original emphasis). Places are temporary and arbitrary achievements.

This approach provides interesting ways to consider the import ascribed to the neighbourhood school in a marketised policy realm. As noted in Chapter 3, the movement of students in and out of catchment areas, enabled through policies of open enrolment, could be seen to dislocate the neighbourhood school. However, neighbourhoods, and neighbourhood schools, as provisional accomplishments of interrelations and negotiations governed in part by the cartography of catchment areas, refuse the categorisation of dislocation. Therefore, the combination of catchment areas and open enrolment compels a reconsideration of the nature of place making. Place is not denied by education markets, rather it is reconfigured. When catchment areas are porous, the neighbourhood school, simplistically yet crucially, is as much a set of practices around, for example, racialised choices, as it denotes a cartographic location.

Furthermore, school choice, as a set of uncertain and unsettling practices, can also lead to conflating educational concerns, risk and uncertainties

(Ball 2003), with broader concerns about the nature of the city. I am thinking here of schools located in areas that are racially marked as dangerous, the way rationalities of fear, or 'spatial anxiety' (Hesse 1997) about race, become a part of schooling . This anxiety elides other fears about the racialised other in the city with fears about schooling success, life trajectories, and so forth. Conceivably, to make sense of the performative aspects of racism and markets requires a conception of place that acknowledges conflict and negotiation, and the possibility of pernicious and unpalatable provisional accommodations.

INVISIBILITY, PERSONAL PREFERENCES AND RACIAL NEOLIBERALISM

Essentially, race inequality in education has continued to persist because social and educational policy has never seriously prioritized its eradication. Rather, policymakers have paid most attention to social control, assimilation and pandering to the feelings and fears of White people. (Gillborn 2008: 86)

In this book I have tried to be attentive to the ways neoliberal education policy reconfigures the relationships between individuals (including parents, students, teachers, and administrators) and the state. I have also been intrigued by how education policy reconfigures relationships between schooling and the city, in Sydney, London, and Vancouver. While there are substantive political, historical, and geographical differences between these three cities, there are also compelling commonalities. These include practices associated with neoliberal education policy that emphasise and constitute the desirability of, and provide available discourses to be taken up by, the aspirational, entrepreneurial self. What is also common to the policies and policy directions examined in this book, Sydney's *Building the Future*, London's *Excellence in Cities*, and school choice policies in Vancouver, is the conspicuous absence of any mention of race or ethnicity. Yet as the preceding chapters have established, race is produced by, and constitutive of, the processes and practices of education policy in inner cities. Race is demonstrably present, yet seemingly rendered invisible. In this section I explore this paradox through the interplay of depoliticisation (Brown 2006), the privatisation of difference, and racial neoliberalism (Goldberg 2009).

Market rationalities and technologies are pervasive features of the education policies examined in this book. In these policies any concerns about equity, which admittedly are few, are framed as a lack of teaching resources narrowing of curriculum provision, the opportunity for all students to have aspirations and improve educational standards, or the opportunity for parents to choose a school for their children. These policies illustrate how neoliberalism incorporates other seemingly oppositional discourses such as equity (Davies and Petersen 2005) to reshape policy 'not by entirely eliminating equity concerns but rather by embedding them within choice and accountability frameworks' (Forsey et al. 2008: 15). This reshaping can also be understood in reference to marketisation as a form of depoliticisation. This:

> involves removing a political phenomenon from comprehension of its *historical* emergence and from a recognition of the *powers* that produce and contour it. No matter its particular form and mechanics, depoliticization always eschews power and history in representation of its subject. (Brown 2006: 15, original emphasis)

The result is that a political phenomenon, like an education market, becomes naturalised. The parent is always a willing consumer of schooling, or the East End or Aboriginal student is always, or always should be, an entrepreneurial, aspirational citizen. The only legitimate and intelligible options, and reasons for success or failure, are individual agency or contingency for 'the powers constitutive of these relations, endeavours, and needs vanish from view' (Brown 2006: 18). Market policies thus shroud the myriad ways the governmentalised state continues to legitimate and consolidate the position of dominant groups, such as the white middle classes.

Neoliberal policy also depends on a depoliticisation of space and place, which obscures conflicts, negotiations, and accommodations. In a depoliticised policy environment what can be ignored is how markets reconfigure place. Moreover, what can be denied are the consequences of place making: whether this be who is deemed to belong; or who is deemed to need to change, to become aspirational, in order to continue to belong; or who is deemed to belong, just not here. For example, while the position of Aboriginal students in inner Sydney was clearly problematic, as evidenced by the closure of certain schools with high proportions of Aboriginal students, the *Building the Future* policy made no mention of how racism may have affected the enrolments at these schools. When Aboriginal students were mentioned in the policy, it was related to the proposal to open a nominally Aboriginal school to be named 'Wingara'; a perverse suggestion redolent of the 'colonial present' (Gregory 2004).

Privatising Difference

Neoliberal education policy valorises the realms of individualisation and responsibilisation, while avowing any role in either producing or ameliorating racialised difference. Brown (2006), in her critique of calls for tolerance, notes that what is significant about these calls is 'its routine privatization of sites of difference' (p. 88). Through privatisation, difference is no longer part of the public sphere rather it is reduced to problems of 'culture'

or 'nature'. Similarly, Goldberg (2009) suggests, in reference to South
Africa, that:

> [w]ithin the state, race has been socially desacrilized, rendered part of
> the profane. . . . But . . . it has hardly disappeared. Rather it has been
> placed behind a wall of private preference expressions of privatized
> choice. The more robustly neoliberal the state, accordingly, the more
> likely race would be rendered largely immune from state intervention
> so long as having no government force behind it. (p. 334)

I am not suggesting that Sydney, London, or Vancouver have the same histories and geographies of race relations as South Africa. Nonetheless, I do
want to work with the idea of expressions of privatised choice.

Neoliberal policies provide available discourses to be taken up by desiring, entrepreneurial subjects. Aspirations and responsibilities circulate
as part of education markets in inner city areas; and the racialisation of
desires and concerns can be diluted by recourse to, for example, discourses
of responsible, rational parenting. Parents in East Vancouver can be committed to the idea of an edgy multicultural community or neighbourhood,
which exists often in the abstract, and yet also committed to the choice of a
primarily white school like Queen Victoria Annex. This choice is partially
framed as concern about the quality of education for their child if other students, such as non-English speaking or ESL students, were provided with
extra resources that divert teacher attention away from their children. As
such, there is a quite strange inversion of affirmative action and an invok-
ing of positive discrimination. Goldberg (2009) notes, in reference to this
occurring in the United States, that '[l]iberalism's very instrument for undo-
ing the effects of racism became neoliberalism's poster child for the condition of racism itself' (p. 337).

Neoliberal policy discourses comprise and make available what is intelligible and allowable; they allow discerning and desiring neoliberal subjects
to gloss over race and racism, by recourse to the realm of personal preferences. It is not racism to want to take care of a child's education, even if this
choice is enmeshed in decisions about the relative unsuitability of 'other'
children as a peer group. Goldberg suggests:

> [i]n diluting, if not erasing race in all public affairs of the state, neolib-
> eral proponents nevertheless seek to privatize racisms alongside most
> everything else. They seek, that is, to protect preference determination
> and expression behind a wall of privacy, untouchable by state inter-
> vention, the outcome of which is to privatize race-based exclusions.
> (Goldberg 2009: 339)

Whiteness as enabled through policy, but never explicated in policy, means
personal preferences are uncoupled from power relations that constitute

race and racism. Policy in a neoliberal context is perhaps 'indifferent to difference' (Petersen and Davies forthcoming), for it must remain anodyne in matters of race, lest it draw attention to the inefficiency of the state as a population technology. Additionally, it must allow scope for manoeuvre; any hint of choice being circumscribed would be tantamount to a policy oxymoron (C. Symes, personal correspondence, 2010). In neoliberal policy discourses then, race is not absent, but invisible (Goldberg 2009). Policy here is colour-blind (Leonardo 2009), and racism is not called to account. However, this does not mean the performative aspects of race cease to circulate. The invisibleness of race operates to maintain and consolidate racism through policy as depoliticised. To recognise this is to posit education policy as a component, and as constituent, of racial neoliberalisms (Goldberg 2009).

EDUCATION POLICY AND A CITY OF WHITENESS

> Standing here, as immune to the cold as a marble statue, gazing towards Charlotte Street, towards a foreshortened jumble of façades, scaffolding and pitched roofs, Henry thinks the city is a success, a brilliant invention, a biological masterpiece—millions teeming around the accumulated and layered achievements of the centuries, as though around a coral reef, sleeping, working, entertaining themselves, harmonious for the most part, nearly everyone wanting it to work. (McEwan 2005: 5)

> Neoliberalism is naïve because it imagines that it is no longer necessary to provide solutions to social questions, that they too will be dissolved as well as the division between the private spheres of the market and the sphere of public authority. Advanced liberal societies will have to face up to the problems of the forms of inequality and poverty generated by these contrived markets and the absence of those capacities to exercise choice within these markets by certain sectors of the population. (Dean 1999: 207)

In this book I have wanted to engage with a sensibility expressed by Amin and Thrift (2002), who note the 'difference it makes to visualize the city as a process, without the pretence of total sight or generalization' (p. 26). This sensibility precludes coming to definitive ideas about the relations between education policy and the contemporary city. In various parts of this book I could be talking about the global city, the neoliberal city, the gentrifying city, the postcolonial city, and the settler city. Sydney, Vancouver, and London can also be posited as multicultural cities, in which different people encounter and interact with each other everyday, in multiple ways that require no references to the white middle classes (e.g., Hage 1998, Keith 2005).

Nonetheless, on the basis of the policy analyses outlined in this book it it seems incumbent upon me to conclude that, while perhaps nearly everyone wants the city to 'work', neoliberal education policies portend inner cities that work, but only for some. The programmes, rationalities, and technologies of neoliberal governmentalities, manifest and operable through education policy, seem to inexorably instantiate the prevalence and precedence of white, middle-class imaginaries in the inner city.

Neoliberal governmentality in reference to education governs through the identification of communities of choice, as the 'means' not just the 'territory' of government (Miller and Rose 2008). This is not the death of the social but a 'metamorphosis' into a form of governing that is predicated on the market (Dean 1999). In the creation of community through the market, it is possible to see how neoliberal policies provide the conditions of possibility that reinforce the idea of people wanting to be, or have their children be around 'people like us'. A commonality albeit crudely, arbitrarily, unified through marketisation. In relation to the ideas of whiteness examined in this book, this could be extended to consider the idea of white aspiration (Hage 1998), that is to want to be both *around* 'people like us' and for 'people to *be* like us'. The white middle classes may thus be positioned as an assemblage of aspiration and idealisation that comprises a city of whiteness (cf. Shaw 2007).

When all is said and done, I am a despairing optimist which is probably why I undertake social policy research. Nonetheless, to my mind, neoliberal education policies, that consolidate and constitute *neoliberal racisms*, augur poorly for the future of inner city areas. The interdependence of policy manifestations and enduring aspects and the mutability of race points, I think, to a likely future for inner cities as racialised places. It is an urban future in which neoliberal policy, rationally deranged in its production of differentiation and naïve in its concealing of difference, is a fast forward button to social Darwinism.

Notes

NOTES TO THE FOREWORD

1. Here I use the 'collective Black' to signify the multiplicity of urbans of color, such as the pathologized African American ghetto, the foreignized Asian American enclaves, and 'illegalized' Latino barrios.

NOTES TO CHAPTER 1

1. I use the word 'public' as a synonym for 'government' and 'state', in reference to schooling (e.g., 'public schools').
2. All participants in the studies included in this book were provided consent letters that made clear no real names of participants would be used. However, the letters also acknowledged insiders could identify participants. It will become apparent that in this book I use the actual names of schools and areas of the city. Naming schools complicates anonymity, but the alternative of not naming schools and areas of the city would mean abstracting space and place, which would defeat part of my argument: that it matters where educational policy unfolds.
3. To that end, this book is a reflection on, a reworking, and an extension of, writing I have undertaken both independently and in collaboration with my colleagues Colin Symes and Robert Parkes.
4. This phrase from Derrida's (1976) *Of Grammatology*, appears thus: "*There is nothing outside the text* [there is no outside-text; *il n'y a pas de hors-texte*]" (p. 158).
5. Liberal in the British Columbian context means socially progressive with some fiscal conservatism, though arguably this government is more neoliberal due to its privatisation agenda.
6. I thank Tim Butler for this framing.
7. I thank Colin Symes for this phrasing.

NOTES TO CHAPTER 3

1. I do not use quotation marks around race as I do not feel the need to mark race as different from other social categories and relations, such as gender, class, and disability, that are rarely bounded by quotation marks (see Leonardo 2009).

NOTES TO CHAPTER 4

1. In 2001, in the inner city areas of Redfern and Waterloo, 41.6 percent and 92.2 percent of people, respectively, lived in public housing (Australian Bureau of Statistics, 2001).
2. The transcripts of these proceedings were publicly available on the NSW Parliament website.
3. Vincent Lingari was a Gurindji man who led a 'walk off', or stop-work action, at the Wave Hill pastoral station in the Northern Territory. This walk off protested wages and conditions for Aboriginal employees on pastoral stations. However, it had a much broader effect. In what is seen as a central symbolic act concerning the issue of land rights in Australia, in 1975 Prime Minister Gough Whitlam poured the local sand of the Wave Hill station into Vincent Lingari's hand, thus handing back the Wave Hill station to the Gurindji people.
4. The Gadigal clan of the Darug Nation are the traditional owners of the land, or 'country', now known as Redfern. Throughout the twentieth century, Aboriginal peoples from regional and remote areas made their way to Redfern and Waterloo, as a consequence of both forced removal from traditional lands and for other reasons such as economic considerations. As such there are many different Aboriginal language groups that reside in inner Sydney. The numerically dominant group in Redfern and Waterloo is the Waradjuri peoples from western NSW. I use the word Aboriginal to describe all language groups and Torres Strait Islanders.
5. *Terra nullius* refers to the colonial assertion that Australia was 'vacant land' when invaded and settled by the British. The myth was formally put to rest with the Mabo vs Queensland (No 2) case in 1992 in which the High Court dismissed the notion of *terra nullius* and recognised Native Title.
6. In late 2004 the NSW government, concurrent with making claims of mismanagement of the AHC, created the Redfern–Waterloo Authority that would effectively take over control of the Block. This control would mean that the AHC would relinquish administration of the Block and that a variety of conditions would be imposed on tenants, including threats to evict those that used drugs. In 2006, in part as a response to the establishment of the Authority, the AHC proposed the Pemulway Project, to be funded independently of the state, and to include an Indigenous college, gym, and other public amenities, as well as housing. In 2008, this proposal was still to be approved by the state government, who, under the Redfern–Waterloo Authority, had final development approval. The planning minister indicated that he, personally, was unlikely to support this plan. On July 8, 2009, permission was finally granted by the Labor government for the Pemulway Project to commence.
7. In yet another instance of ghosts from the past (and present), in 2006 the St Andrews Cathedral School in Sydney proposed to build an Indigenous–only school in Redfern.
8. In the Alexandria Park Community School 2008 Annual Report, 45 percent of students were reported to be in these selective streams, effectively creating a school within a school.

NOTES TO CHAPTER 5

1. This department is now the Department for Children, Schools and Families.
2. The Poplar zone has now been discontinued.

3. White according to the Office of National Statistics.
4. Citigroup is now known as Citi.
5. This section intersperses interview transcripts, field notes, a brief set of contextualisation, and photographs. Photographs can be interpreted according to context, in a similar manner to written texts, as different viewers invest different meanings in the same photographs. Similarly, the actual way photographs are employed depends on context. As such, photographs, in a similar vein to the interview transcripts, both augment, and are an integral part of, the narrative in this section (Pink 2001).
6. The Citigroup Foundation is the philanthropic arm of Citigroup, or now Citi, that in 2002 distributed over US$77.7 million to organisations around the world. US$25,000 for literacy and technology at Bygrove Primary School is listed in the Citigroup Foundation Annual Report for 2006.

NOTES TO CHAPTER 6

1. A research focus on an elementary, rather than a secondary, school market is unusual. The nearest elementary school to residence has been seen as an acceptable option for most parents, due to small sizes, encouraged normative behaviours, and travel considerations. However, elementary schools are increasingly used, as they were sparingly used previously, as part of strategic preparation for certain types of selective or desirable secondary schooling (Ball et al. 1995, Campbell et al. 2009).
2. Urban renewal is a dangerous term in North America, with its connotations of clearing the inner city of people of colour, for 'it was not for nothing that civil rights groups in 1960s America proclaimed "urban renewal = nigger removal"' (Keith 2005: 25).
3. Queen Victoria Annex parents and students benefit from funding Grandview receives as a designated 'needy inner city school'. This includes funding to operate a full-time kindergarten. Previously only those students who were Aboriginal, 'special need', or a recent immigrant qualified for all day kindergarten/day care. With changes to the rules for inner city schools the Annex, and *all* the parents, also receive the 'benefits' of inner city poverty—free kindergarten because of the feeder school arrangement between Grandview and Queen Victoria.

References

Agnew, J. (2005) Space: Place. In Cloke, P. & Johnston, R. (Eds.) *Spaces of geographical thought: Deconstructing human geography's binaries*. London, SAGE Publications.

Allen, J. (2003) *Lost geographies of power*. Oxford, Blackwell.

———. (2004) The whereabouts of power: Politics, government and space. *Geografiska Annaler*, 86 B, 19–32.

Allen, R. L. (1999) The socio-spatial making and marking of 'us': Toward a critical postmodern spatial theory of difference and community. *Social Identities*, 3, 249–277.

Alpin, G. (2000) From colonial village to world metropolis. In Connell, J. (Ed.) *Sydney: The evolution of a world city*. Melbourne, Oxford University Press.

Althusser, L. (1976) *Essays in self-criticism*. G. Lock (Trans). London, Humanities Press.

Amin, A. & Thrift, N. (2002) *Cities: Reimagining the urban*. Cambridge, Polity Press.

Anderson, J. E. (1984) *Public policy making: An introduction,* Boston, Houghton Mifflin.

Anderson, K. J. (1993) Constructing geographies: 'Race', place and the making of Sydney's Aboriginal Redfern. In Jackson, P. & Penrose, J. (Eds.) *Constructions of race, place and nation*. London, UCL Press.

———. (2000) Thinking 'postnationally': Dialogue across multicultural, indigenous and settler spaces. *Annals of the Association of American Geographers*, 90, 381–391.

Anyon, J. (1997) *Ghetto schooling: A political economy of urban educational reform*. New York, Teachers College Press.

———. (2005a) *Radical possibilities: Public policy, urban education, and a new social movement*. New York, Routledge.

———. (2005b) What 'counts' as educational policy? Notes toward a new paradigm. *Harvard Educational Review*, 75, 65–88.

Apple, M. W. (2001) *Educating the 'right' way: Markets, standards, god and inequality*. London, RoutledgeFalmer.

Argent, N. (2005) The neoliberal seduction: Governing-at-a-distance, community development and the battle over financial services provision in Australia. *Geographical Research*, 43, 29–39.

Armstrong, F. (2003) *Spaced out: Policy, difference and the challenge of inclusive education*. London, Kluwer Academic Publishers.

———. (2007) Disability, education, and space: Some critical reflections. In Gulson, K. N. & Symes, C. (Eds.) *Spatial theories of education: Policy and geography matters*. New York, Routledge.

Arum, R. (2000) Schools and communities: Ecological and institutional dimensions. *Annual Review of Sociology,* 26, 395–418.

Australian Bureau of Statistics (2001) 2001 Census basic community profiles and snapshots: State suburbs. Available http: <http://www.abs.gov.au/Ausstats/abs%40census.nsf/Census_BCP_SS_ViewTemplate!ReadForm&Start=1&Count=250&Expand=1> (accessed March 4, 2003).

Bacchi, C. (2000) Policy as discourse: What does it mean? Where does it get us? *Discourse: Studies in the Cultural Politics of Education,* 21, 45–57.

Ball, S. J. (1990) *Politics and policy making in education: Explorations in policy sociology.* London, Routledge.

———. (1994a) *Education reform: A critical and post-structural approach.* Philadelphia, Open University Press.

———. (1994b) Some reflections on policy theory: A brief response to Hatcher and Troyna. *Journal of Education Policy,* 9, 171–182.

———. (1995) Intellectuals or technicians? The urgent role of theory in educational studies. *British Journal of Educational Studies,* 43, 255–271.

———. (1998) Big policies/small world: An introduction to international perspectives in education policy. *Comparative Education,* 34, 119–130.

———. (2000) Performativities and fabrications in the education economy: Towards the performative society. *Australian Educational Researcher,* 27, 1–23.

———. (2003) *Class strategies and the education market: The middle classes and social advantage.* London, RoutledgeFalmer.

———. (2006) *Education policy and social class: The selected works of Stephen J. Ball.* London, Routledge.

———. (2007) *Education plc: Understanding private sector participation in public sector education.* London, Routledge.

———. (2008) *The education debate.* Bristol, The Policy Press.

Ball, S. J., Bowe, R. & Gewirtz, S. (1995) Circuits of schooling: A sociological exploration of parental choice in social class contexts. *Sociological Review,* 43, 52–78.

Barman, J. (1991) Deprivatizing private education: The British Columbia experience. *Canadian Journal of Education,* 16, 12–31.

Barnett, C., Clarke, N., Cloke, P. & Malpass, A. (2008) The elusive subjects of neo-liberalism. *Cultural Studies,* 22, 624–653.

BC Passport (2009) Vancouver's Commercial Drive. Available http: <http://www.bcpassport.com/vancouver-activities/commercial-drive.aspx> (accessed May 16, 2009).

Bird, J. (1993) Dystopia on the Thames. In Bird, J., Curtis, B., Putnam, T., Robertson, G. & Tickner, L. (Eds.) *Mapping the futures: Local cultures, global change.* London, Routledge.

Biskup, P. (1982) Aboriginal history. In Osborne, G. & Mandle, W. F. (Eds.) *Aboriginal history: Studying Australia today.* Sydney, George Allen & Unwin.

Blackmore, J. (2002) Restructuring public schooling: A commentary on the New South Wales proposal *Building the Future. Journal of the HEIA,* 9, 37–46.

Blake, A. (2008) The Thames Gateway Bridge: A 'new' solution to an old problem. In Cohen, P. & Rustin, M. J. (Eds.) *London's Turning: The Making of Thames Gateway.* Aldershot, Ashgate Publishing.

Bondi, L. (2005) Working the spaces of neoliberal subjectivity: Psychotherapeutic technologies, professionalisation and counselling. *Antipode,* 37, 497–514.

Bowe, R., Ball, S. J. & Gold, A. (1992) *Reforming education and changing schools: Case studies in policy sociology.* London, Routledge.

Bradford, M. (1990) Education, attainment and the geography of choice. *Geography,* 75, 3–16.

Brenner, N. & Theodore, N. (2002) Cities and the geographies of 'actually existing neoliberalism'. *Antipode,* 34, 349–379.

————. (2005) Neoliberalism and the urban condition. *City,* 9, 101–107.

British Columbia Ministry of Education (1996 (2001)) School Act: Part 2–Students and Parents. Victoria, British Columbia, Ministry of Education.

————. (2008) School Data Summary 2002/03–2006/07 Queen Victoria Annex. Victoria, British Columbia, Ministry of Education.

Brown, W. (2003) Neo-liberalism and the end of liberal democracy. *Theory and Event,* 7. Available http: <http://muse.jhu.edu/journals/theory_and_event/v007/7.1brown.html>.

————. (2006) *Regulating aversion: Tolerance in the age of identity and empire.* Princeton, N.J., Princeton University Press.

Bulosan, C. (1973) *America is in the heart.* Seattle, University of Washington Press.

Buras, K. (2010) Counterstories on pedagogy and policy making: Coming of age in the privatized city. In Buras, K. with Randels, J., ya Salaam, K. and Students at the Center (Eds.), *Pedagogy, policy, and the privatized city: Stories of dispossession and defiance from New Orleans.* New York, Teachers College Press.

Burchell, G. (1996) Liberal government and techniques of the self. In Barry, A., Osborne, T. & Rose, N. (Eds.) *Foucault and political reason: Liberalism, neoliberalism and rationalities of government.* Chicago, University of Chicago Press.

Burke, C. & Grosvenor, I. (2008) *School.* London, Reaktion.

Butler, J. (1993) *Bodies that matter: On the discursive limits of 'sex'.* New York, Routledge.

Butler, T. & Robson, G. (2001) Social capital, gentrification and neighbourhood change in London: A comparison of three south London neighbourhoods. *Urban Studies,* 38, 2145–2162.

————. (2003) *London calling: The middle classes and the re-making of inner London.* Oxford, Berg.

Byrne, P. J. (2003) Two cheers for gentrification. *Howard Law Review,* 46, 405–432.

Calvino, I. (1972) *Invisible cities.* London, Harcourt.

Campbell, C., Proctor, H. & Sherington, G. (2009) *School choice: How parents negotiate the new school market in Australia.* Sydney, Allen & Unwin.

Castells, M. (1977) *The urban question: A Marxist approach.* London, Edward Arnold.

Choo, C. (2004) *Mission girls: Aboriginal women on Catholic missions in the Kimberley,* Claremont, University of Western Australia Press.

Citigroup (2003) Financial Data. New York, Citigroup Financial Group.

Citigroup Foundation (2003) 2002 Annual Report. New York, Citigroup Foundation.

Clegg, S. R. (1989) *Frameworks of power.* London, Sage Publications.

Cochrane, A. (2007) *Understanding urban policy: A critical approach.* Oxford, Blackwell Publishing.

Cohen, P. (1988) The perversions of inheritance. In Cohen, P. (Ed.) *Multi-racist Britain.* London, Macmillan.

————. (1997) Out of the melting pot into the fire next time: Imagining the East End as city, body, text. In Westwood, S. & Williams, J. (Eds.) *Imagining cities: Scripts, signs, memory.* London, Routledge.

Connell, R. (2007) *Southern theory.* Cambridge, Polity.

Crang, M. & Thrift, N. (2000) Introduction. In Crang, M. & Thrift, N. (Eds.) *Thinking Space.* London, Routledge.

Cresswell, T. (2004) *Place: A short introduction,* Oxford, Blackwell Publishing.

Cruickshank, B. (1993) Revolutions within: Self-government and self-esteem. *Economy and Society,* 22, 327–344.

————. (1994) The will to empower: Technologies of citizenship and the war on poverty. *Socialist Review,* 23, 29–55.

Darcy, M. (2000) Housing: The great divide. In Connell, J. (Ed.) *Sydney: The evolution of a world city.* Melbourne, Oxford University Press.

Davies, B. & Petersen, E. B. (2005) Neo-liberal discourse in the Academy: The forestalling of (collective) resistance. *Learning and Teaching in the Social Sciences*, 2, 77–98.

Davies, S. & Aurini, J. D. (2008) School choice as concerted cultivation: The case of Canada. In Forsey, M., Davies, S. & Walford, G. (Eds.) *The globalisation of school choice*. Oxford, Symposium Books.

Davis, M. (1998) *City of quartz: Excavating the future in Los Angeles*. London, Pimlico.

Dean, M. (1999) *Governmentality: Power and rule in modern society*, Thousand Oaks, CA, Sage Publications.

Dean, M. & Hindess, B. (1998) Introduction: Government, liberalism, society. In Dean, M. & Hindess, B. (Eds.) *Governing Australia: Studies in contemporary rationalities of government*. Cambridge, Cambridge University Press.

Delaney, D. (2002) The space that race makes. *The Professional Geographer*, 54, 6–14.

Deleuze, G. & Guattari, F. (1987) *A thousand plateaus: Capitalism and schizophrenia*, Minneapolis, University of Minneapolis Press.

Department for Education and Skills (2003a) EiC: Excellence in Cities: FAQ. Available http: <http://www.standards.dfes.gov.uk/excellence/faq/?faq=#FAQ2> (accessed July 28, 2003).

———. (2003b) Excellence in Cities. Available http: <http://www.standards.dfes.gov.uk/excellence/> (accessed May 19, 2003).

Derrida, J. (1976) *Of grammatology*. Baltimore, Johns Hopkins University Press.

Desena, J. N. (2006) 'What's a mother to do?': Gentrification, school selection, and the consequences for community cohesion. *American Behavioral Scientist*, 50, 241–257.

Dickson, M. & Power, S. (2001) Education Action Zones: A new way of governing education? *School Leadership and Management*, 21, 137–141.

Dikeç, M. (2007) Space, governmentality, and the geographies of French urban policy. *European Urban and Regional Studies*, 14, 277–289.

Dowling, R. (2009) Geographies of identity: Landscapes of class. *Progress in Human Geography*, 33, 833–839.

Dwyer, O. J. & Jones, J. P. (2000) White socio-spatial epistemology. *Social & Cultural Geography*, 1, 209–222.

Dye, T. R. (1992) *Understanding public policy*. Englewood Cliffs, N.J., Prentice Hall.

Eade, J. (1997) Reconstructing places: Changing images of locality in Docklands and Spitalfields. In Eade, J. (Ed.) *Living the global city*. London, Routledge.

———. (2000) *Placing London: From imperial capital to global city*. Oxford, Berghahn Books.

Easton, D. (1953) *The political system*. New York, Knopf.

Ellsworth, E. (2005) *Places of learning: Media, architecture, pedagogy*. London, Routledge.

———. (2008) Review of Gulson, K. N. & Symes, C. (2007). *Spatial theories of education: Policy and geography matters*. New York: Routledge. *Teachers College Record*, <http://www.tcrecord.org> ID Number: 15247 (accessed January 6, 2009).

Farrar, M. (1997) Migrant spaces and settlers' time: Forming and de-forming an inner city. In Westwood, S. & Williams, J. (Eds.) *Imagining cities: Scripts, signs, memory*. London, Routledge.

Fenton, J. & Myers, J. (2006) Gifted and talented case study: Alexandria Park Community School. Sydney, New South Wales Department of Education and Training.

Flyvberg, B. (2001) *Making social science matter: Why social inquiry fails and how it can succeed again.* Cambridge, Cambridge University Press.

Foley, G. (2001) Black power in Redfern 1968–1972. Available http: <http://www.kooriweb.org/foley/essays/essay_1.html > (accessed March 12, 2007).

Forsey, M., Davies, S. & Walford, G. (2008) The globalisation of school choice? An introduction to key issues and concerns. In Forsey, M., Davies, S. & Walford, G. (Eds.) *The globalisation of school choice.* Oxford, Symposium.

Foster, J. (1999) *Docklands: Cultures in conflict, worlds in collision.* London, UCL Press.

Foucault, M. (1980) *Power/ knowledge: Selected interviews and other writings 1972–1977,* C. Gordon (Ed.). New York, Pantheon Books.

———. (1986) Of other spaces. *Diacretics,* 16, 22–27.

———. (1988) Technologies of the self. In Martin, L. H., Gutman, H. & Hutton, P. H. (Eds.) *Technologies of the self: A seminar with Michel Foucault.* Amherst, University of Massachusetts Press.

———. (1991) *The order of things: An archaeology of the human sciences.* New York, Vintage.

———. (1994a) Governmentality. In Faubion, J. (Ed.) *Power: Essential works of Foucault 1954–1984.* London, Penguin.

———. (1994b) Questions of method. In Faubion, J. (Ed.) *Power: Essential works of Foucault 1954–1984.* London, Penguin.

———. (1994c) The subject and power. In Faubion, J. (Ed.) *Power: Essential works of Foucault 1954–1984.* London, Penguin.

———. (1994d) Truth and power. In Faubion, J. (Ed.) *Power: Essential works of Foucault 1954–1984.* London, Penguin.

———. (2004) *Security, territory, population: Lectures at the Collège de France 1977–1978.* New York, Palgrave MacMillan.

Gale, T. (2001) Critical policy sociology: Historiography, archaeology and genealogy as methods of policy analysis. *Journal of Education Policy,* 16, 379–393.

Gamage, D. T. (1992) School-centred educational reforms of the 1990s: An Australian case study. *Educational Management Administration Leadership,* 20, 5–14.

Gamarnikow, E. & Green, A. G. (1999) The Third Way and social capital: Education Action Zones and a new agenda for education, parents and community? *International Studies in Sociology of Education,* 9, 3–21.

Gewirtz, S. (2001) Cloning the Blairs: New Labour's programme for the re-socialization of working-class parents. *Journal of Education Policy,* 16, 365–378.

Gibson, A. & Asthana, S. (2000) Local markets and the polarization of public-sector schools in England and Wales. *Transactions of the Institute of British Geographers,* 25, 303–319.

Gibson, W. (1984) *Neuromancer.* New York, Ace Books.

Gillborn, D. (2008) *Racism and education: Coincidence or conspiracy?* London, Routledge.

———. (2010a) The colour of numbers: Surveys, statistics and deficit thinking about race and class. *Journal of Education Policy,* 25, 251–274.

———. (2010b) The white working class, racism and respectability: Victims, degenerates and interest-convergence. *British Journal of Educational Studies,* 58, 3–25.

Gillborn, D. & Kirton, A. (2000) White heat: Racism, under-achievement and white working-class boys. *International Journal of Inclusive Education,* 4, 271–288.

Gillborn, D. & Youdell, D. (2000) *Rationing education: Policy, practice, reform and equity.* Buckingham, Open University Press.

———. (2009) Critical perspectives on race and schooling. In Banks, J. A. (Ed.) *The Routledge international companion to multicultural education.* New York, Routledge.

112 *References*

Gilroy, P. (2000) *Against race: Imagining political culture beyond the color line,* Cambridge, Mass., Harvard University Press.

Goldberg, D. T. (2009) *The threat of race: Reflections on racial neoliberalism,* Oxford, Wiley-Blackwell.

Gorard, S. & Fitz, J. (1998) The more things change . . . the missing impact of marketization. *British Journal of Sociology of Education,* 19, 365–376.

Gordon, C. (1994) Introduction. In Faubion, J. D. (Ed.) *Power: Essential works of Foucault 1954–1984.* London, Penguin.

Grace, G. (Ed.) (1984a) *Education and the city: Theory, history and contemporary practice.* London, Routledge & Kegan Paul.

———. (1984b) Theorising the urban: Some approaches for students of education. In Grace, G. (Ed.) *Education and the city: Theory, history and contemporary practice,* London, Routledge & Kegan Paul.

———. (1984c) Urban education: Policy science or critical scholarship? In Grace, G. (Ed.) *Education and the city: Theory, history and contemporary practice.* London, Routledge & Kegan Paul.

———. (1995) *School leadership: Beyond educational management. An essay in policy scholarship.* London, Falmer.

Gregory, D. (1994) *Geographical imaginations.* Oxford, Blackwell.

———. (2004) *The colonial present.* Oxford, Blackwell.

Greyell, E. M. (2001) School history of Grandview and Woodland elementary schools: 1905–1965. In Lee, I. S. & MacFarlan, J. (Eds.) *Grandview/ ?Uuqinak'Uuh Elementary School: History, memories and reminiscences, 1926–2001.* Vancouver, s.n.

Gruenewald D. (2003) The best of both worlds: A critical pedagogy of place. *Educational Researcher,* 32, 3–12.

Gulson, K. N. (2005) Renovating educational identities: Policy, space and urban renewal. *Journal of Education Policy,* 20, 147–164.

———. (2007) Repositioning schooling in inner Sydney: Urban renewal, an education market and the 'absent presence' of the 'middle classes'. *Urban Studies,* 44, 1377–1391.

Gulson, K. N. & Parkes, R. J. (2009) In the shadows of the mission: Education policy, urban space and the 'colonial present' in Sydney. *Race, Ethnicity and Education,* 12, 267–280.

———. (2010a) Bringing theory to doctoral research. In Thomson, P. & Walker, M. (Eds.) *The Routledge doctoral student's companion: Getting to grips with research in education and the social sciences.* London, Routledge.

———. (2010b) From the barrel of the gun: Policy incursions, land and Aboriginal peoples in Australia. *Environment and Planning A,* 42, 300–313.

Gulson, K. N. & Symes, C. (2007) Knowing one's place: Educational theory, policy and the spatial turn. In Gulson, K. N. & Symes, C. (Eds.) *Spatial theories of education: Policy and geography matters.* New York, Routledge.

Gupta, A. & Ferguson, J. (1997) Beyond 'culture': Space, identity, and the politics of difference. In Gupta, A. & Ferguson, J. (Eds.) *Culture, power, place: Explorations in critical anthropology.* Durham, N.C., Duke University Press.

Habermas, J. (1987) *The philosophical discourse of modernity.* Cambridge, Mass., MIT Press.

Hackworth, J. (2007) *The neoliberal city: Governance, ideology, and development in American urbanism,* Ithaca, Cornell University Press.

Hage, G. (1998) *White nation: Fantasies of white supremacy in a multicultural society.* Sydney, Pluto Press.

———. (2005) A not so multi-sited ethnography of a not so imagined ethnography. *Anthropological Theory,* 5, 463–475.

Hall, S. (1997) Cultural identity and diaspora. In Mongia, P. (Ed.) *Contemporary postcolonial theory: A reader.* London, Arnold.

Hall, S. (2007) Housing, regeneration and change in the UK: Estate regeneration in Tower Hamlets, East London. In Beider, H. (Ed.) *Neighbourhood renewal & housing markets: Community engagements in the US & UK.* Oxford, Blackwell.

Harvey, D. (1989) *The condition of postmodernity.* Cambridge, MA, Blackwell.

———. (2005) *A brief history of neoliberalism.* Oxford, Oxford University Press.

Hatcher, R. & Troyna, B. (1994) The 'policy cycle': A Ball by Ball account. *Journal of Education Policy,* 9, 155–170.

Haymes, S. (1995) *Race, culture and the city: A pedagogy for Black urban struggle.* Albany, State University of New York Press.

Henig, J., Hula, R., Orr, M., and Pedescleaux, D. (2001) *The color of school reform: Race, politics, and the challenge of urban education.* Princeton, Princeton University Press.

Hesse, B. (1997) White governmentality: Urbanism, nationalism, racism. In Westwood, S. & Williams, J. (Eds.) *Imagining cities: Scripts, signs, memory.* London, Routledge.

Howlett, M. & Ramesh, M. (1995) *Studying public policy: Policy cycles and policy subsystems.* Oxford, Oxford University Press.

Hubbard, P. (2006) *City.* London, Routledge.

Hubbard, P., Kitchin, R. & Valentine, G. (2004) Editor's introduction. In Hubbard, P., Kitchin, R. & Valentine, G. (Eds.) *Key thinkers on space and place.* London, Sage Publications.

Human Rights and Equal Opportunity Commission (1997) *Bringing them home: Report of the national inquiry into the separation of Aboriginal and Torres Strait Islander children from their families.* Sydney, Human Rights and Equal Opportunity Commission.

Humes, W. & Bryce, T. (2003) Post-structuralism and policy research in education. *Journal of Education Policy,* 18, 175–187.

Jenkins, R. (2003) Rethinking ethnicity: Identity, categorization, and power. In Stone, J. & Dennis, R. M. (Eds.) *Race and ethnicity: Comparative and theoretical approaches.* Malden, Mass., Blackwell.

Jones, K. (2003) *Education in Britain: 1944 to present.* Cambridge, Polity Press.

Jones, M. (2009) Phase space: Geography, relational thinking, and beyond. *Progress in Human Geography,* 33, 487–506.

Jull, P. (2004) While Redfern riots, Whites do battle. *Arena Magazine* 70, 22.

Keith, M. (2005) *After the cosmopolitan? Multicultural cities and the future of racism.* London, Routledge.

Keith, M. & Cross, M. (1993) Racism and the postmodern city. In Cross, M. & Keith, M. (Eds.) *Racism, the city and the state.* London, Routledge.

Keith, M. & Pile, S. (1993) Conclusion: Towards new radical geographies. In Keith, M. & Pile, S. (Eds.) *Place and the politics of identity.* London, Routledge.

Kelley, R. (1998) *Yo' Mama's disfunktional!: Fighting the culture wars in urban America.* Boston, Beacon Press.

Kenway, J. & Bullen, E. (2001) *Consuming children: Education-entertainment-advertising.* Buckingham, Open University Press.

Knox, P. L. (1995) World cities in a world-system. In Knox, P. L. & Taylor, P. J. (Eds.) *World cities in a world-system.* Cambridge, Cambridge University Press.

Larner, W. (2000) Neo-liberalism: Policy, ideology, governmentality. *Studies in Political Economy,* 63, 5–25.

Leander, K. M. & Sheehy, M. (Eds.) (2004) *Spatializing literacy research and practice.* New York, Peter Lang.

Leaside Regeneration Ltd (2003) Leaside SRB4: Year 5 delivery plan 2002/2003. London, Unpublished.

Lee, I. S. & MacFarlan, J. (Eds.) (2001) *Grandview/ ?Uuqinak'Uuh Elementary School: History, memories and reminiscences, 1926–2001,* Vancouver, s.n.

Lees, L. (2003) Policy (re)turns: Gentrification research and urban policy, gentrification and urban policy. *Environment and Planning A, 35,* 571–574.

———. (2008) Gentrification and social mixing: Towards an inclusive urban renaissance? *Urban Studies, 45,* 2449–2470.

Lees, L., Slater, T. & Wyly, E. (2008) *Gentrification.* New York, Routledge.

Lefebvre, H. (1991) *The production of space.* Oxford, Blackwell.

Leonardo, Z. (2002) The souls of white folk: Critical pedagogy, whiteness studies, and globalization discourse. *Race, Ethnicity and Education, 5,* 29–50.

———. (2009) *Race, whiteness, and education.* New York, Routledge.

———. (2010) Whiteness and New Orleans: Racio-economic analysis and the politics of urban space: Afterword to Buras, K. with Randels, J., ya Salaam, K. and Students at the Center (Eds.), *Pedagogy, policy, and the privatized city: Stories of dispossession and defiance from New Orleans.* New York, Teachers College Press.

Leonardo, Z. & Hunter, M. (2007) Imagining the urban: The politics of race, class and schooling. In Pink, W. T. & Noblit, G. W. (Eds.) *International handbook of urban education.* Dordrecht, Springer.

Levin, B. (2009) Enduring issues in urban education. *Journal of Comparative Policy Analysis: Research and Practice, 11,* 181–195.

Levine-Rasky, C. (2008) Middle-classness and whiteness in parents' responses to multiculturalism: A study of one school. *Canadian Journal of Education, 31,* 459–490.

Ley, D. (1996) *The new middle class and the remaking of the central city,* Oxford, Oxford University Press.

Ley, D. & Dobson, C. (2008) Are there limits to gentrification? The contexts of impeded gentrification in Vancouver. *Urban Studies, 45,* 2471–2498.

Lingard, B. (2000) Federalism in schooling since the Karmel Report (1973). *Australian Educational Researcher, 27,* 25–61.

Lingard, B. & Ozga, J. (2007) Introduction: Reading educational policy and politics. In Lingard, B. & Ozga, J. (Eds.) *The RoutledgeFalmer reader in education policy and politics.* London, Routledge.

Lipman, P. (2007) Education and the spatialization of urban inequality: A case study of Chicago's Renaissance 2010. In Gulson, K. N. & Symes, C. (Eds.) *Spatial theories of education: Policy and geography matters.* New York, Routledge.

———. (2008) Mixed-income schools and housing: Advancing the neoliberal urban agenda. *Journal of Education Policy, 23,* 119–134.

Lipsitz, G. (2007) The racialization of space and the spatialization of race: Theorizing the hidden architecture of landscape. *Landscape Journal, 26,* 10–23.

Longhurst, R. (2003) Introduction: Subjectivities, spaces and places. In Anderson, K. J., Domash, M., Pile, S. & Thrift, N. (Eds.) *Handbook of cultural geography.* London, Sage Publications.

Lucey, H. & Reay, D. (2002) A market in waste: Psychic and structural dimensions of school-choice policy in the UK and children's narratives on 'demonized' schools. *Discourse: Studies in the Cultural Politics of Schooling, 23,* 253–266.

Lupton, R. (2009) Area-based initiatives in English education: What place for place and space. In Raffo, C., Dyson, A., Gunter, H., Hall, D., Jones, L. & Kalambouka, A. (Eds.) *Education and poverty in affluent countries.* Abingdon, Routledge.

Lupton, R. & Tunstall, R. (2008) Neighbourhood regeneration through mixed communities: A 'social justice dilemma'? *Journal of Education Policy, 23,* 105–117.

Mackey, E. (1999) *The house of difference: Cultural politics and national identity in Canada.* New York, Routledge.

Marginson, S. (1997a) *Educating Australia: Government, economy and citizen since 1960.* Cambridge, Cambridge University Press.

———. (1997b) *Markets in education.* St Leonards, Sydney, Allen & Unwin.

Marston, G. & McDonald, C. (2006) Introduction: Reframing social policy analysis. In Marston, G. & McDonald, C. (Eds.) *Analysing social policy: A governmental approach*. Cheltenham, Edward Elgar.

Massey, D. (1993a) Politics and space/time. In Keith, M. & Pile, S. (Eds.) *Place and the politics of identity*. London, Routledge.

———. (1993b) Power-geometry and a progressive sense of place. In Bird, J., Curtis, B., Putnam, T., Robertson, G. & Tickner, L. (Eds.) *Mapping the futures: Local cultures, global change*. London, Routledge.

———. (1994a) Double articulation: A place in the world. In Bammer, A. (Ed.) *Displacements: Cultural identities in question*. Bloomington, Indiana University Press.

———. (1994b) *Space, place and gender*. Cambridge, Polity.

———. (2005) *For space*. London, Sage Publications.

———. (2007) *World city*. Cambridge, Polity.

Massey, D. and Denton, N. (1993) *American apartheid*. Cambridge, MA, Harvard University Press.

McDowell, L. (1999) *Gender, identity and place: Understanding feminist geographies*, Minneapolis, University of Minnesota Press.

McEwan, I. (2005) *Saturday*. Toronto, Alfred A. Knopf.

McGregor, J. (2004) Space, power and the classroom. *Forum: For promoting 3–19 comprehensive education*, 46, 13–18.

Miller, P. & Rose, N. (2008) *Governing the present: Administering economic, social and personal life*. Cambridge, Polity Press.

Morgan, G. (2006) *Unsettled places: Aboriginal people and urbanisation in New South Wales*. Kent Town, Wakefield Press.

Mosca, E. & Spicer, V. (2008) 2007 Commercial Drive Community Survey. Vancouver, ICURS, Simon Fraser University.

Murdoch, J. (2006) *Post-structuralist geography: A guide to relational space*. London, Sage Publications.

Nayak, A. (2004) White lives. In Murji, K. & Solomos, J. (Eds.) *Racialization: Studies in theory and practice*. Oxford, Oxford University Press.

———. (2006) After race: Ethnography, race and post-race theory. *Ethnic and Racial Studies*, 29, 411–430.

Nerlich, G. (1994) *The Shape of Space*. Cambridge, Cambridge University Press.

New South Wales Department of Education and Training (2001a) Building the Future: An education plan for inner Sydney (draft proposal). Sydney, New South Wales Department of Education and Training.

———. (2001b) Building the Future: Consultation report. Sydney, New South Wales Department of Education and Training.

New South Wales Parliament Legislative Council: General Purpose Standing Committee No 1 (2002a) Proposed closure and restructuring of inner Sydney schools. Sydney, New South Wales Parliament Legislative Council.

———. (2002b) Report of 7th June 2002 proceedings before inquiry into the proposed closure and restructuring of government schools in inner Sydney. Sydney, New South Wales Parliament Legislative Council.

———. (2002c) Report of 29th May 2002 proceedings before inquiry into the proposed closure and restructuring of government schools in inner Sydney. Sydney, New South Wales Parliament Legislative Council.

———. (2002d) Report of 31 May 2002 proceedings before inquiry into the proposed closure and restructuring of government schools in inner Sydney. Sydney, New South Wales Parliament Legislative Council.

New South Wales Teachers Federation (2002) Submission to Legislative Council: Inquiry into the proposed closure and restructuring of government schools in inner Sydney. Available http: <http://www.nswtf.org.au/dp_extras/Future1.pdf> (accessed January 26, 2007).

O'Flynn, G. & Petersen, E. B. (2007) The 'good life' and the 'rich portfolio': Young women, schooling and neoliberal subjectification. *British Journal of Sociology of Education,* 28, 459–472.

Office for Standards in Education (2003a) Excellence in Cities and Education Action Zones: Management and impact. London, OFSTED Publications Centre.

———. (2003b) Inspection report: Bygrove Primary School. London, Office for Standards in Education.

Office of National Statistics (2001) Neighbourhood statistics: Statistics by area. Available http: <http://neighbourhood.statistics.gov.uk/area_select_fs.asp?nsid =false&CE=True&SE=True> (accessed March 5, 2003).

Olssen, M., Codd, J. & O'Neill, A. M. (2004) *Education policy: Globalization, citizenship and democracy.* London, Sage Publications.

Orsini, M. & Smith, M. (2007) Critical policy studies. In Orsini, M. & Smith, M. (Eds.) *Critical policy studies.* Vancouver, UBC Press.

Osborne, T. & Rose, N. (1999) Governing cities: Notes on the spatialisation of virtue. *Environment and Planning D: Society and Space,* 17, 737–760.

Ozga, J. (1987) Studying education policy through the lives of policy makers. In Walker, S. & Barton, L. (Eds.) *Changing policies, changing teachers.* Milton Keynes, Open University Press.

———. (2000) *Policy research in educational settings: Contested terrain.* Buckingham, Open University Press.

Pal, L. A. (1987) *Public policy analysis: An introduction,* Toronto, Methuen.

Peck, J. & Tickell, A. (2002) Neoliberalising space. *Antipode,* 34, 380–404.

Peters, M. A. (2009) Introduction: Governmentality, education and the end of neoliberalism? In Peters, M. A., Besley, A. C., Olssen, M., Maurer, S. & Weber, S. (Eds.) *Governmentality studies in education.* Rotterdam, Sense Publishers.

Peters, M. A. & Humes, W. (2003) Editorial: The reception of post-structuralism in educational research and policy. *Journal of Education Policy,* 18, 109–113.

Peters, M. A. & Kessl, F. (2009) Space, time, history: The reassertion of space in social theory. *Policy Futures in Education,* 7, 20–30.

Petersen, E. B. (2004) Academic boundary work: The discursive constitution of 'scientificity' amongst researchers within the social sciences and humanities. Department of Sociology. Copenhagen, PhD No.25, University of Copenhagen.

———. (2009) Resistance and enrolment in the enterprise university: An ethno-drama in three acts, with appended reading. *Journal of Education Policy,* 24, 409–422.

Petersen, E. B. & Davies, B. (forthcoming) In/ Difference in the neoliberal university. *Learning and Teaching in the Social Sciences.*

Petersen, E. B. & O'Flynn, G. (2007) Neoliberal technologies of subject formation: A case study of the Duke of Edinburgh's award scheme. *Critical Studies in Education,* 48, 197–211.

Pettman, J. (1995) Race, ethnicity and gender in Australia. In Stasiulis, D. & Yuval-Davis, N. (Eds.) *Unsettling settler societies: Articulations of gender, race, ethnicity and class.* London, Sage Publications.

Pink, S. (2001) *Doing visual ethnography.* London, Sage Publications.

Pink, W. T. & Noblit, G. W. (Eds.) (2007) *International handbook of urban education,* Dordrecht, Springer.

Popkewitz, T. S. (1998) *Struggling for the soul: The politics of schooling and the construction of the teacher.* New York, Teachers College Press.

Poplar Zone (2000) The Poplar zone: Application to establish a small Education Action Zone. London, Unpublished.

Port Jackson District Office (2003) Port Jackson school district enrolments. Sydney, Unpublished.

Power, S., Rees, G. & Taylor, C. (2005) New Labour and educational disadvantage: The limits of area-based initiatives. *London Review of Education,* 3, 101–116.

Power, S., Warren, S., Gillborn, D., Clark, A., Thomas, S. & Coate, K. (2002) *Education in deprived areas: Outcomes, inputs and processes*. London, Institute of Education, University of London.

Power, S., Whitty, G., Gewirtz, S., Halpin, D. & Dickson, M. (2004) Paving a third way? A policy trajectory analysis of Education Action Zones. London, Education and Social Research Council.

Price, G. (2005) *Price tags*. Vancouver, Sightline Institute.

Probyn, E. (2003) The spatial imperative of subjectivity. In Anderson, K.J., Domash, M., Pile, S. & Thrift, N. (Eds.) *Handbook of cultural geography*. London, Sage Publications.

Raco, M. (2009) From expectations to aspirations: State modernisation, urban policy, and the existential politics of welfare in the UK. *Political Geography*, 28, 436–444.

Raffo, C. & Dyson, A. (2007) Full service extended schools and educational inequality in urban contexts—New opportunities for progress? *Journal of Education Policy*, 22, 263–282.

Razack, S. H. (2002) When place becomes race. In Razack, S. H. (Ed.) *Race, space and the law*. Toronto, Between the Lines.

Reay, D. (2007) 'Unruly places': Inner city comprehensives, middle-class imaginaries and working class children. *Urban Studies*, 44, 1191–1201.

———. (2008) Class out of place: The white middle classes and intersectionalities of class and 'race' in urban state schooling in England. In Weis, L. (Ed.) *The way class works: Readings on school, family, and the economy*. New York, Routledge.

Reay, D., Crozier, G., James, D., Hollingworth, S., Williams, K., Jamieson, F. & Beedal, P. (2008) Re-invigorating democracy?: White middle class identities and comprehensive schooling. *The Sociological Review*, 56, 238–255.

Reay, D., Hollingworth, S., Williams, K., Crozier, G., Jamieson, F., James, D. & Beedel, P. (2007) 'A darker shade of pale?': Whiteness, the middle classes and multi-ethnic inner city schooling. *Sociology*, 41, 1041–1060.

Redfern Waterloo Partnership Project (2003) RWPP Newsletter October 2003. Sydney, Redfern Waterloo Partnership Project.

Reid, A. (2005) The regulated education market has a past. *Discourse: Studies in the Cultural Politics of Education*, 26, 79–94.

Richardson, T. & Jensen, O. B. (2003) Linking discourse and space: Towards a cultural sociology of space in analysing spatial policy discourses. *Urban Studies*, 40, 7–22.

Rizvi, F. & Lingard, B. (2009) *Globalizing educational policy*. London, Routledge.

Robertson, S. L. (2009) Spatialising the sociology of education: Stand-points, entry-points, vantage-points. Available http: <http://www.bris.ac.uk/education/people/academicStaff/edslr/publications/28slr> (accessed November 22, 2009).

Robinson, J. (2006) *Ordinary cities: Between modernity and development*. London, Routledge.

Robson, G. & Butler, T. (2001) Coming to terms with London: Middle class communities in a global city. *International Journal of Urban and Regional Research*, 25, 70–86.

Rose, N. (1996) Governing 'advanced' liberal democracies. In Barry, A., Osborne, T. & Rose, N. (Eds.) *Foucault and political reason: Liberalism, neo-liberalism and rationalities of government*. London, UCL Press.

Ross, A. (2002) A representative profession? Ethnic minority teachers. In Johnson, M. & Hallgarten, J. (Eds.) *From victims of change to agents of change: The future of the teaching profession*. London, Institute for Public Policy Research.

Said, E. (1978) *Orientalism*. London, Penguin Books.

———. (1983) *The world, the text, and the critic*. Cambridge, Mass., Harvard University Press.

———. (1993) *Culture and imperialism*. New York, Vintage Books.

Sassen, S. (1991) *The global city: New York, London, Tokyo.* Princeton, N.J., Princeton University Press.

Saul, J. R. (2005) *The collapse of globalism and the reinvention of the world.* Camberwell, Vic., Penguin.

Scheurich, J. (1994) Policy archaeology: A new policy studies methodology. *Journal of Education Policy,* 9, 297–316.

Seaborne, M. (1971) *The English school: Its architecture and organisation 1370–1870,* London, Routledge & Kegan Paul.

Sennett, R. (1999) Growth and failure: The new political economy and its culture. In Featherstone, M. & Lash, S. (Eds.) *Spaces of culture: City, nation, world.* London, SAGE Publications.

Sharkansky, I. (1970) *Policy analysis in political science.* Chicago, Markham.

Shaw, W. S. (2000) Ways of whiteness: Harlemising Sydney's Aboriginal Redfern. *Australian Geographical Studies,* 38, 291–305.

———. (2006) Decolonizing geographies of whiteness. *Antipode,* 38, 851–869.

———. (2007) *Cities of whitness.* Oxford, Blackwell Publishing.

Shields, R. (2006) Knowing space. *Theory, Culture and Society,* 23, 147–149.

Simons, H. (1996) The paradox of case study. *Cambridge Journal of Education,* 26, 225–240.

Simons, M., Olssen, M. & Peters, M. A. (2009a) Re-reading education policies: Part 1: The critical policy orientation. In Simons, M., Olssen, M. & Peters, M. A. (Eds.) *Re-reading education policies: A handbook studying the policy agenda of the 21ˢᵗ century.* Rotterdam, Sense Publishers.

———. (2009b) Re-reading education policies: Part 2: Challenges, horizons, approaches, tools, styles. In Simons, M., Olssen, M. & Peters, M. A. (Eds.) *Re-reading education policies: A handbook studying the policy agenda of the 21ˢᵗ century.* Rotterdam, Sense Publishers.

Smith, M. P. (2001) *Transnational urbanism: Locating globalisation.* Oxford, Blackwell.

Smith, N. (2002) New globalism, new urbanism: Gentrification as global urban strategy. *Antipode,* 34, 427–450.

———. (2004) Space and substance in geography. In Cloke, P., Crang, P. & Goodwin, M. (Eds.) *Envisioning human geographies.* London, Arnold.

Smith, R. G. (2007) Poststructuralism, power and the global city. In Taylor, P., Derudder, B., Saey, P. & Witlox, F. (Eds.) *Cities in globalization: Practices, policies and theories.* London, Routledge.

Soja, E. W. (1989) *Postmodern geographies: The reassertion of space in critical social theory,* New York, Verso.

———. (1996) *Thirdspace: Journeys to Los Angeles and other real-and-imagined places,* Cambridge, Mass., Blackwell.

South Sydney City Council (2003) Redfern Waterloo community profile. Sydney, Unpublished.

Sparke, M. (2005) *In the space of theory: Postfoundational geographies of the nation-state.* Minneapolis, University of Minnesota Press.

Statistics Canada (2008) Canada's ethnocultural mosaic, 2006 Census: Canada's major census metropolitan areas. Available http: <http://www12.statcan.ca/census-recensement/2006/as-sa/97–562/p24-eng.cfm> (accessed April 2, 2010).

———. (2010) Visible minority: Definition. Available http: <http://www.statcan.gc.ca/concepts/definitions/minority-minorite1-eng.htm> (accessed March 30, 2010).

Stoney, S., West, A., Kendall, L. & Morris, M. (2002) Evaluation of Excellence in Cities: Overview of interim findings. London, Excellence in Cities Evaluation Consortium.

Symes, C. (2007a) Coaching and training students: An ethnography of students commuting on Sydney's suburban trains. *Mobilities,* 2, 443–461.

———. (2007b) On the right track: Railways and schools in late nineteenth century Sydney. In Gulson, K. N. & Symes, C. (Eds.) *Spatial theories of education: Policy and geography matters*. New York, Routledge.

Tamboukou, M. & Ball, S. J. (2003) Genealogy and ethnography: Fruitful encounters or dangerous liaisons? In Tamboukou, M. & Ball, S. J. (Eds.) *Dangerous encounters: Genealogy and ethnography*. New York, Peter Lang.

Taylor, C. (2002) *Geography of the 'new' education market: Secondary school choice in England and Wales*, Hampshire, Ashgate.

———. (2007) Geographical information systems (GIS) and school choice: The use of spatial research tools in studying educational policy. In Gulson, K. N. & Symes, C. (Eds.) *Spatial theories of education: Policy and geography matters*. New York, Routledge.

———. (2009a) Choice, competition, and segregation in a United Kingdom education market. *American Journal of Education*, 115, 549–568.

———. (2009b) Towards a geography of education. *Oxford Review of Education*, 35, 651–669.

———. (2010) The globalisation of school choice? *Globalisation, societies and education*, 8, 163–166.

Taylor, S., Rizvi, F., Lingard, B. & Henry, M. (1997) *Educational policy and the politics of change*. London, Routledge.

Thiem, C. H. (2007) The spatial politics of educational privatization: Re-reading the US homeschooling movement. In Gulson, K. N. & Symes, C. (Eds.) *Spatial theories of education: Policy and geography matters*. New York, Routledge.

———. (2008) Thinking through education: The geographies of contemporary educational restructuring. *Progress in Human Geography*, 33, 154–173.

Thomson, P. (2002) *Schooling the rustbelt kids: Making the difference in changing times*. Stoke on Trent, Trentham Books.

———. (2007) Working the in/visible geographies of school exclusion. In Gulson, K. N. & Symes, C. (Eds.) *Spatial theories of education: Policy and geography matters*. New York, Routledge.

Thrift, N. (2006) Space. *Theory, Culture & Society*, 23, 139–155.

Tikly, L. (2003) Governmentality and the study of education policy in South Africa. *Journal of Education Policy*, 18, 161–174.

Tower Hamlets Council (2004) Strategic plan for the education service 2002–2006. London, Tower Hamlets Council.

———. (2006) Tower Hamlets vision for building schools for the future (draft). London, Tower Hamlets Council.

Tower Hamlets Local Education Authority (2003) Achieving against the odds: The challenge. Available http: <http://www.towerhamlets-pdc.org.uk/policies.php?id=12> (accessed May 21, 2003).

Tupechka, T., Martin, K. & Douglas, M. (1997) *Our own backyard: Walking tours of Grandview Woodland*. Vancouver, Simon Fraser University.

Urry, J. (2003) Social networks, travel and talk. *British Journal of Sociology*, 54, 155–175.

Usher, R. (2002) Putting space back on the map: Globalisation, place and identity. *Educational Philosophy and Theory*, 34, 41–55.

Vancouver School Board (1989 (Revised 2003)) School Attendance Areas (Boundaries). Vancouver, Vancouver School Board.

———. (1989 (Revised March 3 2003)) School Attendance Areas (Boundaries). Available http: <http://www.vsb.bc.ca/districtinfo/policies/j/jcschoolattendanceareas.htm> (accessed March 15, 2009).

Veracini, L. (2003) The evolution of historical redescription in Israel and Australia: The question of the 'founding violence'. *Australian Historical Studies*, 34, 326–345.

Vidovich, L. (2007) Removing policy from its pedestal: Some theoretical framings and practical possibilities. *Educational Review, 59,* 285–298.

Vinson, T. (2002) Inquiry into the provision of public education in NSW: Report of the 'Vinson Inquiry'. Sydney, Pluto Press.

Walks, R. A. & Maaranen, R. (2008) The timing, patterning, and forms of gentrification and neighbourhood upgrading in Montreal, Toronto, and Vancouver,1961 to 2001. Toronto, Centre for Urban and Community Studies, Cities Centre, University of Toronto.

Waller, W. (1937) *The sociology of teaching.* New York, Wiley.

Warde, A. (1991) Gentrification as consumption: Issues of class and gender. *Environment and Planning: Society and Space, 6,* 75–95.

Warf, B. & Arias, A. (2009) Introduction : The reinsertion of space in the humanities and social sciences. In Wark, B. & Arias, S. (Eds.) *The spatial turn: Interdisciplinary perspectives.* Abingdon, Routledge.

Webb, P. T. (2005) The anatomy of accountability. *Journal of Education Policy, 20,* 189–208.

———. (2006) The choreography of accountability. *Journal of Education Policy, 21,* 201–214.

Webber, R. & Butler, T. (2007) Classifying pupils by where they live: How well does this predict variations in their GCSE results. *Urban Studies, 44,* 1229–1253.

Whitty, G. (1997) Creating quasi-markets in education: A review of recent research on parental choice and school autonomy in three countries. *Review of Research in Education, 22,* 3–47.

Windle, J. (2009) The limits of school choice: Some implications for accountability of selective practices and postional competition in Australian education. *Critical Studies in Education, 50,* 231–246.

Wright, E. O. (2005) Conclusion: If 'class' is the answer, then what is the question? In Wright, E. O. (Ed.) *Approaches to class analysis.* Cambridge, Cambridge University Press.

Yoon, E. & Gulson, K. N. (2010) School choice in the 'stratilingual' city of Vancouver. *British Journal of Sociology of Education, 31.*

Youdell, D. (2004) Engineering school markets, constituting schools and subjectivating students: The bureaucratic, institutional and classroom dimensions of educational triage. *Journal of Education Policy, 19,* 407–431.

———. (2006) *Impossible bodies, impossible selves: Exclusions and student subjectivities.* Dordrecht, Springer.

Young, R. J. C. (1990) *White mythologies: Writing history and the west.* London, Routledge.

Index